CONVERSATIONS WITH Gurudev

VOLUME I

MAHĀMANDALESHWAR SWAMI NITYĀNANDA

Copyright © 2016 Shanti Mandir

ISBN 978-0-9886025-7-1

Shanti Mandir
51 Muktananda Marg
Walden, NY 12586, U.S.A.

Tel: +1 (845) 778–1008
www.shantimandir.com

Conversations without beginning or end...

Oftentimes in our conversations we reach a certain point where we say, "Okay, period. Full stop." When we do this, there can be no further conversation, no further dialogue. We put a stop to it because we don't want to deal with our issues. It's too painful. It hurts. We don't like it. One thing is certain: the day we die, there will be no further conversations. So, at least while we are living, we can have conversations. If we're willing to listen, to ponder and imbibe the teachings, fresh questions will arise. This makes a conversation exciting. And it can continue. And continue. Instead of a period, we just put a comma.

 *Gurudev*

TABLE OF CONTENTS

Preface ix
Putting Water Back in the Ocean 1
Meditate on Your Self 3
Present in Every Moment. 7
The Play of Māyā. 17
Surrender Happens Automatically Within 21
Love Is Already There 25
Whatever Takes Place Is What You Need to Experience. . . . 29
Don't Let Your Mind Trick You. 37
A Golden Vessel. 41
The Light Shines Through 45
The Mantra Redeems. 49
All This Is a Reflection 53
We Are All Light 61
The Point of Meditation. 65
Practice Has to Be Alive 69
Personal Daily Practice 73
Where the Soul Goes 77
Grace Is Always There. 81
Never Miss a Day. 85
The Best Redemption. 89
Be Who You Are 93
Fill Their Hearts. 99
God's Wife 103
Winding Down. 105
Draw Wisdom Through Your Love 109
Nature Takes Care of Itself 113
What Type of Disciple Are You? 117
Fast Yoga 125
Honor the Divinity Within. 127
Stay Focused 133
The Hundredth Sheep 139
Inner Freedom 143
Voice of the Heart 149
Love Yourself. 153
Simplify Your Life. 157

Larks and Owls	163
The Company of the Truth	165
Forgive and Forget	171
Pillars of Peace	175
Baba Gave Us a Lifestyle	179
Be Doubly Good	189
Through Love, Discipline	197
The Most Amazing Thing	203
We Need to Do More	207
Guru and Disciple	211
Make the Mind Your Servant	221
Intensity of Practice	225
The Breath	229
Filled with Light	233
The Cycle of Reincarnation	239
Become a Gopī	249
The Light of Many Bulbs	253
A Journey of a Few Centimeters	257
The Guru's Job	261
Using the Guru as a Crutch	267
The Origin of Mind	271
Does God Exist?	275
Āratī	279
Power of Mantra	281
The Value of Human Birth	285
The Simplicity of Devotion	293
Sanātan Dharma	297
To Get to the Formless, Start with the Form	301
What is Enlightenment?	303
Emotion Is Energy	307
Be Like a Flute	311
Clarity of Mind	313
Become Waves in the Ocean	319
Hold Your Bliss	323
Live in the World and Practice Yoga	327
Glossary	335

PREFACE

I'm reminded of a story about two stones. There is a temple, and as is the case in most Indian temples, inside is a deity made of a stone. It is smooth white marble, or maybe granite. People go to it to pray or worship, to offer lights, incense, fruits, and flowers. A priest does worship to it all day long. Outside the temple there is another stone, a rough stone. People walk over it. They sit on it. They run into it. People do different things to that stone.

One day, the stone outside has a chat with the stone inside the temple. He complains, "You are a stone. I am a stone. Our basic quality of nature is stone. Yet you are worshipped and everybody thinks you are God. They touch you so delicately. But look at me! People kick me. They spit on me. Little kids do other things. A car bumps into me. So what is the difference between us?"

The stone that has become the deity says, "The difference is that I have survived the chisel. I silently bore the hammering of the artist who carved this deity from stone. As a result, I'm not just a stone anymore. I have taken on divine form. I am worshipped by people who do not think of me as stone, but think of me as divine. Thus I lead them to that experience within."

Many of us go through life being the stone outside. We lie there or sit there, and we get bumped, just like the stone outside. We rarely venture into the temple within. Even if we go to *satsaṅg*, do we really listen to the teachings? And if we listen, do we really ponder them?

I believe we must ponder what we have heard. We must think further, ask ourselves more questions. For example, "Do I believe what was said or do I have to think more about how I understand what was said?"

I can see when people do this. I see the mind trying to figure out "Exactly what did you mean when you said that?" Then you know the person is getting ready with his next questions to ask.

When you read our scriptures—whether it's the *Upaniṣads* or another scripture—you often see that it is nothing but a dialogue between the disciple and the Guru. It is what we might call a question and answer session. In those days, the Guru and disciple lived together for ten, twelve, or fifteen years. The disciples study. They listen. They practice. When a disciple hears a teaching from the Guru, he ponders it for the next few days, or few weeks. Then he comes back wanting to understand it better.

Nowadays, it is the same thing. The disciple visits the Guru, they spend time with each other, and then the disciple goes away and lives his life. Later he comes back and he asks the Guru more questions so he can take the teachings deeper in his own life.

When people came to Baba Muktānanda from the West in the late 1960s early 1970s, everybody wanted to know "What is it that you do?" They were beginning to have spiritual experiences, so they had many questions: "Why is this happening to me? Why is that happening to me? What is this? What is that?" But at that time, there was nobody around to explain what was happening. There were no talks.

People came. People sat. People chanted. People did *sevā*. People went into what even as little children we understood as spontaneous meditation. Nobody told them they would have a *kuṇḍalinī* awakening. They didn't have two months of classes explaining what kuṇḍalinī is and preparing them. They would just come and have out-of-body, out-of-mind experiences. Then they would try to understand what happened to them. What did Muktānanda do?

One of the stories I love is about a young girl who was living in Mumbai. She told her grandmother she had decided to visit Muktānanda.

The grandmother said, "Do you know what will happen?"
The girl said, "Yes."
The grandmother said, "Your life will change."
The girl said, "Yes, I know. Therefore I'm going."
The grandmother said, "Don't say afterwards that I didn't warn you about the effect Muktānanda would have."

I think some part of us loves that experience. We know that is really what we are, and who we are.

So Baba listened to the Westerners' questions, and of course he had answers. The first books he gave us were five volumes of questions and answers from those meetings. These books, the *Satsang with Baba* series, are not available now.

If you read these books, you see that sometimes the same person asks the same question again in a different way. The mind was still trying to understand. It is wondering, "Will he change his answer? Is he going to change what he believes?"

You also find that Baba answers the same question again and again. His thoughts are expressed a bit differently each time because, of course, the question is being asked a bit differently by each person. But, overall, you find that he stays consistent. What he has experienced, what he has found and come to know within himself does not change.

To this day, each person does *sādhanā* at home, in his or her own space. Then we come together in a group and share the great things that are being experienced. We try to understand better what is happening in each one's life.

The scriptures say there are two kinds of questions: questions that are uplifting and beneficial, and questions that are what I call rambling thoughts. The latter don't have a purpose or a focus. The person hasn't understood yet what he wants to know.

Therefore, you must think of three practices from Vedānta: *śravaṇa*, *manana*, and *nididhyāsana*.

Śravaṇa, listen. After having listened, manana, contemplate. Following satsaṅg, sit and contemplate the teachings. You heard the words. But the words are not what remain with you. What remains is the feeling, and that feeling must be contemplated. "How do I understand it?"

Contemplate how the teaching you heard applies to you. Then apply it; use the teaching in your life. What matters is not something somebody said or something you read. What matters is what you have come to know. Nididhyāsana means imbibing the teachings your Guru has given you. Become absorbed in the teachings so they are no longer separate, but are your own direct experience.

Mahāmandaleshwar Swami Nityānanda

PUTTING WATER BACK IN THE OCEAN

Question: In *A Book for the Mind*, Baba said, "When pure Consciousness becomes contracted, it becomes the mind." Can you explain?

Gurudev: I have that book with me, actually. Somebody gave it to me in Florida.

Baba is quoting from the fifth *sūtra* of the *Pratyabhijñā-hṛdayam*, which says that Consciousness contracts and becomes the mind. It limits itself within the body, within the individual.

According to the process described by Kashmir Shaivism, you expand the limited mind again and experience the great Consciousness.

I think the simplest way to understand this is to use the example of the ocean. Imagine that you go to the ocean and fill a mug with water. The water in the mug and the water in the ocean are not different, except that the water in the mug doesn't have sharks or dolphins or seaweed. Therefore, it is a limited version of the water in the ocean.

When you put the water in that mug back into the ocean, once again it becomes one with the ocean. You can no longer distinguish which water was in the mug. It is now all simply the ocean.

In the same way, when the great Consciousness enters the body, the individual identifies with the body. He identifies with the mug. I've been told that in Australia mug means something else. So, let's say he identifies with the cup.

For as long as the individual identifies with the body, Consciousness is limited. It limits itself by imagining, "This is all I can do."

When you're able to become free of the limitations of the body, you experience that same Consciousness as vast. Of course, it's one thing in theory and a different thing in practice.

Question: But is it an attainable goal?

Gurudev: Everything is attainable. One has glimpses at times when one is not caught in one's own limitations.

MEDITATE ON YOUR SELF

Question: Muktānanda said, "Meditate on your Self, bow to your Self, worship your Self. God dwells within you as you." I was wondering if you could address the nature of the Self and how to increase our awareness of it.

Gurudev: As Baba traveled the world, he always reminded everybody that this was his only message. Each of us must come to recognize the divinity that dwells within us.

We want to be the divine Self at all times. That is the understanding and the goal.

At the same time, we all live in this world, and we're all a part of everything that happens in this world. In this way, we get caught in the external aspects of the world.

We become so busy. We have to ask ourselves, "What am I busy doing?" We have technology that is supposed to make life simpler, easier, better, faster. But I'm not so sure that is true. People are driving and texting, or driving and phoning. Often as I travel, each person has an instrument and everybody starts to worry if it hasn't beeped in the last fifteen minutes. So, how has technology made life easier and better?

From childhood till the day they die, people experience their entire world as outside themselves. When you come to satsaṅg, or start to do a personal practice, you want instead to bring your focus within.

The philosophy of Shaivism says, "The focus has to be within." Even while you are operating in this world, the focus cannot be outside, it has to be within.

Baba's Guru, Bhagavān Nityānanda, gave a simple example. All of us eat fruit. The seeds of most fruits are inside the fruit. But one fruit, the cashew nut, has its seed outside the fruit. It's attached to the fruit, but it's not inside the fruit. It remains separate from the fruit. So Bhagavān would say this is how we have to learn to live in the world—not totally lost and immersed in the world. We want to live in the world, yet separate from it.

Many people find this difficult. They ask, "How can I live in the world but be separate from it?"

You can start by making an assessment of how your life is going. I heard somebody mention it is his birthday today. You can take stock at whatever age you are. Look at the memories you have from the past twenty, thirty, forty, fifty years and ask, "Which of these memories do I cherish? Which are of value?" A sage would suggest that most of your memories are pleasurable. They gave you joy or fun in that moment. But think about it: did they give you everlasting joy? Everlasting fun? Probably you would have to say, "It was good then."

Instead, take your focus within. Ask, "What have I done within myself?"

The other day somebody said, "All we need is wisdom."

In my understanding, along with wisdom, each of us needs to look within our individual self. We can't simply say, "Meditate on your Self" and not look at the individual who exists within that divine Consciousness.

Until we become a great sage who is always established in that awareness within, we are human beings who must deal with this world. We have feelings. We have emotions. However, we haven't yet learned to control them.

Baba said, "Meditate on your Self. Honor your Self. Worship your Self. Respect your Self. Love your Self." You have to become clear about what that Self is. You have an individual body, which is how you recognize yourself. This is not the body Baba is talking about. He's talking about the Consciousness that comes into this body and that will one day leave this body and go into some other body. It is that Self, that Consciousness, that must be recognized.

We do recognize it at times. We are aware, but then we forget. We become John again, we become whoever our name or identity is. We forget that we are the big Self.

One of the teachings we heard while we were in Ganeshpuri was *viśala hṛdaya*. A magnanimous heart. Remain big.

By looking within, I have come to realize that the Self is not a part or a piece of Consciousness. Rather, Consciousness is everywhere. It is within that Consciousness that I exist.

The philosophy of Shaivism explains this. When you look at the ocean, you see it has waves. If you are a surfer, you are only interested in the waves. You want to catch a wave. You forget that the ocean is where the waves arise. However, the wave is not separate, not other than the ocean. The wave is the ocean, and the ocean is the wave.

In the same way, you realize you are the ocean of Consciousness. For a moment, it is as if the wave of your individuality arises. And then it merges back. The form with which you identify arises, but really it is Consciousness.

You live in Sydney, by the ocean. Sit by the water and consider how vast the ocean is. As you try to understand what Consciousness is, what the Self is, you can think of the ocean, of the sky.

The scriptures ask, "Where does the sky begin, where does the sky end? Where does the ocean begin, where does the ocean end?"

You have traveled in a boat. I don't think while you were in that boat you would say, "Yes, the ocean begins here" or "The ocean ends here." You understand that the ocean is not just what you can see. It is vast, unlimited.

In the same way, when you begin to comprehend the Self and Consciousness, you consider where it begins and where it ends. That is a good starting point.

PRESENT IN EVERY MOMENT

Question: What is meditation?

Gurudev: Over time, you learn to sit. You sit in one position for at least thirty minutes minimum, to sixty minutes. And you enjoy being able to sit.

Many people feel they want to move after a few minutes. They want to get up, to do something. Therefore, I say the very first thing you need to do is become aware of your posture, and become established in that.

Sitting on a cushion may not feel good. A sofa may not feel good. But if it's a good firm seat, you can sit for one or two hours. There is nothing in the body or the mind that bothers you.

Next you become aware of your breathing. As you focus on the breath, you are able to let go of thoughts. You are able to relax.

Then become aware of the *mantra*. Whether you repeat *Oṁ Namaḥ Śivāya* or you do *Haṁsa* does not matter. Baba always said, "The less you need to repeat it, the better." Because the mantra is just a vehicle that you use to become still and quiet.

In the beginning, all this takes time. But as you become more adept, you are able to move through the initial steps within five or ten minutes. Then you have a full thirty to forty minutes, or longer, during which you are able to sit with no thoughts—or at least with only a few thoughts. You experience a sense of peace.

You become addicted to meditation. Each day you want to sit and experience that peace. On a day that you are too busy or something interferes and you aren't able to meditate, you are aware all day long that you were not able to do it.

Make a routine out of meditation. At the same time, you don't want to see it as something that has to be done. Rather, you want to do it out of love, out of joy.

Then you learn to take that feeling with you throughout the day. You don't leave the stillness wherever you sat in the morning; you carry it with you.

The *Bhagavad Gītā* says, "Yoga is skill in action."

I'll share a story that explains skill in action. Everybody had different work around Baba. Some people were carpenters. Others worked in the kitchen.

One man is in the kitchen, cutting a piece of cucumber. Baba walks up to him and says, "How many slices?" The man thinks, "What do you mean, how many slices? How can I know how many slices are in that cucumber?" Baba looks at him and says, "Thirty." Three zero. Baba takes the knife, and cha-cha-cha, he cuts it. He puts the knife down and tells the man to count.

The man counts. There are only twenty-seven. In that moment he thinks, "Do I lie to the Guru and tell him there are thirty when there are only twenty-seven? Or do I tell him the truth that there are only twenty-seven?" He chooses to tell the truth.

Baba says again, "How many?" Baba was always in a rush, so you only had a split second to think: "How much truth or not truth to tell him?"

The man repeats, "Twenty-seven."

Baba says, "Turn over the knife."

And there are the other three. That makes thirty.

I love this story because this is an expression of what we saw growing up with Baba. You ask, "What does meditation do?" Meditation gives you that laser-sharp brain, those laser-sharp actions.

Around Baba, the opportunity to make mistakes was not there. Either you were with it or you were not with it. We learned that if you wanted to be around Baba and feel good about yourself, you'd better be with it. Otherwise he didn't want you around. You were just a dead weight. You were useless. You were a donkey. You were stupid. And he told you that very clearly.

How did you develop these qualities? You had to develop them through the process of meditation. You had to go inside yourself. He taught you this.

Baba didn't teach us meditation by saying, "Okay, sit, I'll teach you meditation." It happened through everything we did.

All the actions that were performed around him had to have that focus, that skill.

We would sit in the courtyard with Baba in his ashram in India. Our job was to watch him so that when he wanted something, we would be able to deliver it in the next moment. As I said, he was very quick, and he expected us to be quick too.

At the same time, we had to know what was going on in the periphery. We were looking at Baba, but we were also watching what was going on around him. So when he would say, "Go get that one," we knew who it was that he had watched. And we would go and get him.

All this was focus, one-pointedness, meditation. If he asked us to get someone, and we said, "Who?" he would have a nice deluge of words. He would tell us how foolish and stupid and idiotic we were not to be focused and present enough to know whom he wanted.

If you ever thought meditation meant checking out of this world, you simply had to live with Baba for one month. Then you realized that meditation had nothing to do with checking out of this world.

Meditation has to do with being present. Present in every moment. Present in every thought. Present in every action. You do the practice of sitting for an hour a day to be prepared for the next twenty-three hours.

Some people say, "Oh, I'd get tired."

But as we did around Baba, you learn not to get tired. You learn not to operate from the ego, from a sense of smallness or limitedness. You operate from being vast like the sky. Even things you consider inert or dead can talk to you. You learn to talk to and communicate with them.

So to me, meditation is feeling Consciousness in everything. I believe everything is happening simultaneously. It happens in this reality as we know it, at its appointed time. But it has already happened.

For example, think of a child inside its mother's womb. The new life is getting ready. Then in the ninth month, it pops out.

But it doesn't just come into existence on that day. All along it has been preparing.

In the same way, you experience all that is happening in meditation, in Consciousness, before it comes down into the physical level. Meditation teaches you to connect to everything at the level of the unseen truth. Then when something happens on this mundane level, you already know it's going to happen. I've lost you now. Does that make sense?

Question: Is it better to repeat the seed mantras and meditate on the various *chakras* or to continue doing *Haṁsa*?

Gurudev: When you meditate at home, I always suggest doing the *Haṁsa* mantra. The chakra meditation is wonderful to do together as a group. You experience the energy together. But if you try to figure out each chakra's focus as you are meditating at home alone, then the whole sense of one-pointed focus is lost.

When you sit at home every day, first become aware of sitting. Then turn your awareness to the breath. Then add the mantra.

The idea is to come to a place of simple quiet. In that place, there is no mantra. There is nothing.

At some point, you find that place of stillness and quiet. Then more of your time in meditation is spent just sitting in quiet. Maybe a few thoughts are lingering here and there. They aren't important. The stillness, the silence, is what is important.

Question: Often when I'm meditating, I forget to breathe. At what point do I need to be concerned?

Gurudev: Well, perhaps your husband should be concerned. But no, you don't have to be concerned.

The silence and the stillness I talked about are experienced naturally during the retention of breath, or *kumbhaka*. The breath just stops.

In his books, Baba talks about breathing that happens in the *suṣumnā*, the central channel in the subtle body. Breathing is still taking place. Otherwise you would not be alive. It just moves deeper. So you have to become aware of that.

I remember the first time my breath stopped. I was about sixteen or seventeen. I also had the same thought: "I'm going to die because I'm not breathing." But it had been twenty minutes, and I was still alive.

I realized afterwards that was what the sages call *nirvikalpa samādhi*—oneness in which there are no thoughts, there is total stillness.

You are aware of the breathing you do normally through your nostrils. As you come again and again to a place of stillness, you discover your breathing happens deeper inside.

I think it's good. This means you have gone to a deep place, a quiet and still place. So not to worry.

Question: I am wondering if you will describe what it's like for you when you meditate and chant?

Gurudev: It will be fifty years of doing this. Sometimes I ask myself, "When did it begin?" I don't really know. I have often joked that it began inside my mother's womb.

We all come with karma. I think I'm very fortunate that my family already belonged to this lineage. I didn't have to think and ask and worry about it. The path came naturally. The practices came naturally.

Around Baba, you had to get up early. I actually loved getting up early because I loved going to the morning *āratī* to play the gong or the conch. Everybody came to the evening āratī, but not everybody came to the morning āratī. Either they were meditating or sleeping or doing sevā. But for me, getting up early came naturally. And it still does today.

Over the years, I've come to the understanding that meditation is not something you do for just a few moments a day. You have to try to be peaceful throughout the day. Whenever you find yourself agitated, frustrated, or caught in some feeling, you take a few moments to get rid of that.

Growing up with Baba, I saw that he would be sitting in the courtyard for *darśan*. Then all of a sudden, he would get up. It happened totally out of the blue. The darśan line was going, but he would stop it. He would go into his room and sit there for fifteen minutes. Then he would go back to the courtyard.

As a ten-year-old child, I didn't quite understand what Baba did. Of course, people would make up theories. Some thought he went in to meditate so he could contact somebody somewhere. Most people probably thought he went to the bathroom. He didn't. When he went inside, he sat on the little stool in front of his bed. He did what he did, and then he came back out.

Looking back, I realize we all have to learn to do that. Whenever the instinct or desire arises, take a few moments do what needs to be done.

Meditation is about eliminating thoughts.

Throughout the day, you have thoughts. You see. You hear. You read. You have interactions. All of that leaves impressions within you. So you sit quietly. Whether you do the mantra or follow your breath, you try to just let go. You realize you already have all that you want.

As you sit, you become aware of different thoughts and impressions. If you are able to understand them, well and good. If you aren't able to understand, just let them go.

Sometimes people struggle hard to understand what is happening in their minds, in their lives. They feel they have to know, and they have to know now. I think it's not necessary to know now. If you don't understand something, I believe the best is to put it on what I call simmer. Let it sit there, and then later the illumination will come.

If you want to know something, you send out a thought about it. Then just sit or do whatever you do. What you asked about exists somewhere in the cosmos, in the universe. And so the answer comes to you.

Now, you have to trust this answer. You can't think, "Did I imagine that? Did I just have a random thought?" The answer you receive is a result of your offering, your surrender, your dedication to the entire cosmos.

At the same time, you don't have to go around and tell the whole world, "I saw this" or "I know that." It's not necessary. Those who are on the path with you will know and understand. Those who are not on the path will not understand anyway.

Ultimately, meditation is a space of silence. When we were at the Rothko Chapel recently, we heard that Mark Rothko said, "Silence is so accurate."

In Bhagavān Nityānanda's world, silence is silence of the mind.

As you meditate or chant, you become joyous and excited. What you want to do is find the stillness, the silence, that exists in the midst of that excitement.

In the ashram in Magod, the students chant the Vedic mantras. They all sing in one key, one rhythm. Everybody's together, especially when they sing the *Rudram* on Monday mornings. It's a powerful experience to sit there and listen to the one sound for an hour and twenty or thirty minutes. Even if you don't understand the mantras, you can listen to the power of the sound. You realize you've come to a very deep place.

I think of chanting as medicine. When you take physical medicine, it goes wherever the pharmacist or doctor wants it to go. In the same way, the medicine of chanting goes deep within.

As we were chanting *Śrī Rām*, I thought, "It's too bad we have to stop." If we all had agreed and made the adjustment, we could have kept on chanting.

I was reminded of a *sādhu* we visited last year in the Himalayas. It was four o'clock in the afternoon, and about six of us were walking along the Ganges. Somebody told me a sādhu lived there.

As we walked by his little hut, we saw a sign: "Free stay. Free food. You must chant." Chanting was his fee.

Of course, the sādhu came running out. "Swamiji!" He told

everybody to come inside. We had to bend down to get through the door of his hut.

He asked us, "What do you do?"

We told him.

Then he said, "Do you chant?"

We said, "We chant."

He said, "Who plays the drum?"

One person sat down with the drum.

He said, "Okay, I'll make some chai. You chant."

While the chai was cooking, we started to chant.

Then he said, "Who plays the harmonium?"

So the drummer took the harmonium, and somebody else took the drum.

He said, "You chant while I strain the chai."

I think we all should make chanting a natural part of our lives like that. It wasn't "first we will chant, then we will have chai." The chai was being made while the chanting was happening. The chai was being strained, and chanting was still happening. Everything took place, I think, within an hour.

The hut was a very small space. While we were having chai, we asked the sādhu where everybody slept.

He said, "When nobody is here, I sleep in that room." It was maybe eight feet by eight feet. He said, "When I have guests, they sleep in there, and I sleep out here." That space was maybe three by six, just enough for him to lie down.

We create too many ideas about what meditation and chanting are. The theories we create and the concepts we have don't matter. Ultimately, it is just about being simple.

If you were to ask Bhagavān the question you asked me, he would say, "My experience twenty-four hours a day is chanting and meditation. When chanting happens, I enjoy that. When nothing happens, I enjoy that."

We get caught sometimes. Living in the modern world, we compartmentalize so many things. We create all these partitions and divisions. "Now I will be spiritual. Now I will be materialistic. Now I will be good. Now I will be holy. Now I will be a parent.

Now I will be a spouse." We are always trying to figure out which one we are in the moment. This is when *māyīya mala* arises.

You have to dissolve all those differences. That, to me, is what meditation is. Just be yourself. Play the role you play, without getting caught in trying to play that role.

Meditation is becoming a witness, observing all the scenes that take place in your life. Chanting simply adds music to it.

THE PLAY OF MĀYĀ

Question: I've been struggling to understand the nature of separation. I was wondering if you would share your understanding of the malas, and particularly māyīya mala.

Gurudev: It is a veil that comes from the ego. When you think of yourself as good or bad or whatever you feel, then you feel separate. The quality described by māyīya mala is what makes you perceive separation.

In that moment, think to yourself, "Why do I feel like this? Why am I experiencing this?" Both the *Bhagavad Gītā* and the *Bhakti Sūtras* say that māyā is difficult to cross. Because all that you see is nothing but the play of māyā.

As we were driving up the street this morning, I thought to myself, "It's a beautiful day. It's warm. If we told people we'll gather in the park for a picnic, we would get better attendance than we get by saying we'll gather to meditate."

On July 4th at the ashram in Walden, somebody said to me, "Everybody was on time for the picnic. You tell these same people to come on time for the chant or for satsaṅg or for a program, and they will get delayed. But for the picnic," he said, "they were on time, even ahead of time."

I said, "That is māyā—the pleasure of the senses, the pleasure of the mind."

It was the funniest sight, actually. We were playing volleyball, and the potluck lunch was being set up maybe five hundred feet away. People were already waiting in line.

We all know that with potluck, it's a matter of luck. In the beginning, there are maybe fifty dishes. After a few people go through the line, it's down to forty-five or forty. By the end, if you come last, maybe there are only ten. You look at somebody else's plate and ask, "Where did you get that? I didn't see it on the table."

The person says, "I went through the line first."

Somebody sent us a message, "Please stop the game and come so everybody can be together at one time, and everybody gets everything."

I just laughed to myself. I said, "They can start."
But I was told, "No, they want everybody there."
When people think about māyā, they think, "No, no, I'm not so caught in māyā."
We have a book called *The Nectar of Discourses*, written by Swami Maheshwarānanda, who was the Guru of the Mahāmandaleshwar who gave us *sannyāsa*. A man came to Swamiji in Mumbai and said to him, "My family tortures me. I don't do anything for them now because I don't work and earn money anymore. I don't serve a purpose, so they would like to see me die." He didn't use the word *die*, but that's what he meant.
Swamiji said, "Why don't you come and live with us here in the ashram? You can attend morning and evening satsaṅg. You can do some sevā. You can go to the temple. You can chant, you can meditate. And you'll get your meals here."
The man suddenly switched his tone. He said, "Swamiji, why are you speaking against my family?"
Swamiji was surprised. He said, "But you are the one who told me they aren't nice to you. I'm just offering a solution. Here is a place you can stay and nobody will bother you."
Māyā is so strong within us. Whether it is due to laziness or to wanting to do something or not do something, it takes a long time to become aware of the distinctions and separations māyā creates. The only way out is to slowly overcome it each and every time it arises. I think the day that māyā is gone, the whole game is over. At least for that individual.

SURRENDER HAPPENS AUTOMATICALLY WITHIN

Question: How does one surrender?

Gurudev: I remember a particular incident that occurred in 1978. A man came up to Baba, about a month into our stay in Melbourne. He brought his passport, his house keys, his car key—everything. He put all of it on Baba's footstool, which was in front of his throne, and said, "I surrender to you."

Baba said, "Good. Now you can take all your things back."

We always think surrender means giving up our material possessions. Yesterday someone asked me about the statement in the scriptures that says, "Everything you own—your money, your wife, your child, your house—belongs to the Guru, to God." He asked, "Does the scripture really mean this?"

I said, "Yes. When one has the understanding that the Guru and I are one, then there are not two. It follows that everything belongs to that principle, whether we call it the Guru or God."

Of course, the question arises: if it's all one, who provides? We may work for eight or ten hours a day, and we think we're going to get money as compensation. We think, "It's my boss who's giving me the money."

But is it really? Someone who's not separate from us is watching over us to make sure we get that money.

Sometimes when I think of surrender, I think of animals in the wilderness. They live a truly surrendered life, not worrying about tomorrow. From them we can see that true surrender is surrender of the mind, of the ego, of duality, of the sense of separation.

As soon as we think something is "mine" and that "I need to give," we have created duality. But when we have truly surrendered, we see that whatever we think of as "mine" actually belongs to God, to the Guru, or to whomever we regard as our deity.

As our understanding expands, we can better grasp what surrender is. It is not an act that needs to be performed externally; it is something that happens automatically within us. The Indian scriptures contain many stories that talk about God coming in various forms to test His devotees to see how much they have truly surrendered.

Anyway, today you have all surrendered to sitting inside this tent!

LOVE IS ALREADY THERE

Question: Maybe God wants to show us that we have to find something through sorrow, through pain, to be guided back to the love that we can experience. Is this how God teaches us?

Gurudev: I will quote from Kabīr. He says, "Curse that happiness that makes your heart forget God's name; welcome that pain and suffering that compel you to repeat God's name at every moment."

The only problem I sometimes find is that people get too caught up in the sorrow and forget to go for the love. A lady in New York constantly argues with me about this, saying that she's closest to God when she is sorrowful.

But my argument is that it's human nature to prefer the company of someone who is joyous over the company of someone who is sorrowful. If someone is joyful, I want to sit with him or her for hours. But if someone is sorrowful, I might go out of sympathy, but I can't wait to get out of there.

Yes, hard times, pain, and suffering do remind us of God. They remind us to think about the purpose of human life. But sometimes we take this experience too far. How many times do you have to stick your hand in fire before you discover that it burns you?

The scriptures talk about a love that is experienced deep within and doesn't come from ego. Here's how I see the difference between this experience and ordinary love: When I love from my ego, I want that love to be acknowledged. But when the love comes from a deep place, it doesn't matter whether it's acknowledged or not; I still have the feeling of love.

Question: But if you have this true love and just indulge in it, you'll be on your own and isolated. Surely this can't be the goal or the end of the process?

Gurudev: The ones who have experienced this love never really sat isolated. Many went out and were with people. In our time, we can take Mother Teresa as an example. Her love led her to take care of people who couldn't take care of themselves or who were not being taken care of by other people. Her big organization is well set up today, but when she began, I'm sure she had a lot of problems.

Although it seems that a person who becomes immersed in love would be isolated, in reality he or she is not. Such a one realizes that all of what happens in this world is just part of the ongoing cycle of creation, sustenance, and dissolution. When we have this understanding, we are able to sit back and watch—or to step forward and take action—without becoming involved in the cycle.

Question: So, I must find true love within myself, but contentment will only come when I can share this love with other people?

Gurudev: They are both within you. When you share love with people, it only increases the love that is already within you.

It's like putting your money in the bank. You put it in, and then it gives you interest. It's not that the bank will give you money on which to make interest. You've already put it there. In the same way, the love is there within you, and the joy and contentment are there, and they increase when you share them.

Question: So which is more important: having love or giving love?

Gurudev: The most important thing is to feel love. When you have love, then it automatically oozes out of you.

This goes back to what I said earlier. When you have love, people want to come and be with you. It's not that you have to go out and say, "I love, therefore come to me." Because there is love, they automatically come.

Question: It sounds logical that if I have love, I can share love. For me, love is just to accept myself to the fullest extent, which also means accepting the negative side. Everybody has many problems, but to really fully accept oneself, one develops this love.

Gurudev: The love I speak about is already there. It does not need to be found or developed or worked upon.

If in our limited state we share love, certainly it can be helpful. But still, that kind of love comes from ego. In that limited love, if a negative experience were to take place, we would feel hurt. But when we come from the deepest experience of love, we give without expecting any kind of return from the person to whom we give.

Of course, all of us have to accept ourselves as we are. Baba's teaching was "God dwells within you, as you." As we learn to love and accept ourselves, we tap into the love that is already there.

WHATEVER TAKES PLACE
IS WHAT YOU NEED
TO EXPERIENCE

Question: When one first begins sādhanā, there's a lot of excitement. *Kriyās* and visions happen. But later on, in my case anyway, it seems to get a lot more placid. Is this because I'm not striving enough or is it just the natural progression?

Gurudev: The example I use is that when you drive from Delaware to New York, you only go through New Jersey once. And as you go even further north, you don't go into New Jersey again. Similarly, whatever experiences you may have in sādhanā do not repeat themselves.

At the same time, when you begin anything, there is a lot of excitement, enthusiasm. You sit regularly for meditation. You do *japa* regularly. You read the scriptures regularly. The practices are done regularly. Then as time goes on, there's a little bit of slackening. You slip a little bit, and then you pick up your pace again. This up and down, up and down goes on.

At other times, you come to a plateau where nothing seems to be happening. You don't have kriyās or visions. But things start to happen in other parts of your life. Whatever takes place is what you need to experience.

Once there was a man who had been on tour with Baba for a few years. He went up on the darśan line one day, and thought to himself, "All these people get up and give these experience talks about the blue pearl, their visions, the joy and bliss they feel, this and that." As he approached Baba, he made a mental list of the experiences he thought he should have.

Then he bowed and said, "Okay, Baba,"—he didn't say it verbally, just mentally—"these are the things I would like to experience."

Within the next three days he had all the experiences he wanted. And at the end of the last one, Baba came to him in a vision and asked, "Is there anything else you'd like to see?"

The man was blown away. He began to look at his life, and he realized that so much transformation had taken place since he met Baba. Everything that needed to take place had happened.

I was asked to give my first experience talk when I was

fifteen. I went up to my room and I thought, "What am I going to talk about? Am I going to talk about Baba yelling at me? Or am I going to talk about how he brought me up?"

As I sat down and began to think about the years I'd spent around Baba, I began to more fully appreciate all the different things that had occurred.

For this reason, I don't like to tell people what they will experience. A new person who walks in cold has no idea what he or she is walking into. But as soon as this person thinks he or she knows what that experience will be, then the person will look for it. A lot of times, people look for visions in meditation. They want to see lights or hear sounds. Yet, whatever a person has within will manifest, regardless.

In the old days, people sat down and Baba simply walked in. Nobody told you he was going to give you śaktipat. Nobody told you anything about what you'd experience. You just sat there. Often you felt something had happened, but you didn't know what it was. And then you would go to someone you knew and ask, "What was that?" But that person didn't know, either.

It was not until 1970, after Baba wrote *Play of Consciousness*, that people started calling it śaktipat, or kuṇḍalinī awakening, and using all the correct terms. The same experiences had been happening all along, it was just that nobody could say what they were.

Now, because we've read so many books and heard so many talks, we think, "Okay, this is what's happening to me. And I want that to happen too."

But every step along the way in sādhanā, things change. One year, you might be very much into meditation. The next year you might be into japa. The next year you might be into doing nothing, just being silent.

We go through these phases, and each is part of our own unique development. The fact that you don't spend a lot of time meditating during one phase doesn't mean you are no longer into meditation. It's just that meditation has shifted to a different form or a different level of your being.

I think this is one of the tricks Baba liked to play on us. When you first met him, he would give you such a powerful experience that you'd be totally blown away. You'd think, "God, this is great! I'm going to sit for meditation every day, and this is what's going to happen." And then you would sit the next day and nothing would happen.

So I like to think of these experiences as catalysts. They get you going on the path. You're still here, so I think we can say it has worked for you!

Question: What is kuṇḍalinī?

Gurudev: There is energy in this universe, right? That much we all believe. Energy is what makes it all happen.

Sound travels—that's energy. Electricity travels—that's energy. Wind is energy. Fire is energy. Everything is energy.

The same energy that exists outside also dwells within our body in a condensed form. When it dwells within us, the term is kuṇḍalinī.

It is said that it is coiled three and a half times. You can think of it as like a snake, coiled three and a half times at the base of the spine. The word *coil* in Sanskrit is *kuṇḍala*. Because it is feminine, it becomes kuṇḍalinī.

In Sanskrit, there are different names depending on how something is used. For example, water has more than a hundred and fifty. We call it rain water or ocean water or river water. It's still water, but depending on the form, Sanskrit has a different term.

In meditation, your kuṇḍalinī becomes active. And your kuṇḍalinī is not different from all other kuṇḍalinī or from the great energy that exists in this universe.

Question: There are a lot of teachings about chakras, and many include the seventh. I was wondering if you could talk about that.

Gurudev: In our teachings, we are taught only about six chakras. What you refer to as the seventh is considered the crown chakra, or *sahasrāra*, the thousand-petaled lotus. It is said that it is already open. It is already free of impressions, of *saṁskāras*. It is where the union of female and male takes place within the body.

The kuṇḍalinī must pierce through and open the six chakras. These six carry all the various impressions, and they travel with us in our subtle body as we go from body to body after death.

Question: Kuṇḍalinī moves in me quite a bit. Fear comes up, and I'm wanting a little advice about how to stay with it.

Gurudev: A good hatha yoga teacher would help. Hatha yoga does basically the same thing as kuṇḍalinī yoga. It helps to remove blocks. When you meditate after doing hatha yoga, it is easier to release and let go.

Fear comes up because of the unknown. We don't know what is going to happen. So accept that you don't know. Besides, knowing would not help, either.

Question: When I meditate, kuṇḍalinī moves in my body and it's actually fairly pleasant. I can get very distracted by it. Should I try to stop the movements, which then activates my mind, or should I let them happen?

Gurudev: There are various blocks within the body. As the kuṇḍalinī moves, these blocks have to be removed. That's what causes the movements. The best thing is to just allow those movements to take place.

Around Baba, we saw a lot of movements. It happened to people you'd never think would be able to move in that way. When you met them alone or talked to them later, sometimes they were not even aware of all the things that had happened to them.

I remember in Melbourne in 1978, an Australian man was speaking, I think, Japanese or some other language. If you asked him afterwards, "What did you say?" he didn't know. He didn't understand what he was saying.

The best is to forget you are having movements. Just allow yourself to become immersed. Movements will happen, and then some years later you'll miss those movements. This happens sometimes. People say, "I had wonderful visions. I had wonderful movements. But it doesn't happen to me now." They are worried. They wonder if the kuṇḍalinī is not working in them anymore.

We had a joke around Baba. Someone comes up to Baba and says, "I have no more movements."

Baba says, "That means you're all clear. You have no more blocks."

Of course, the person is elated to hear this. It means he's very pure compared with the rest of the crowd.

But suppose Baba says instead, "That means you are so choked up that there's no space for the kuṇḍalinī to move."

Now the person is worried.

So, enjoy your movements. Let them happen. I would say there's a stillness within that movement, as well. That stillness, that energy, is what you want to feel and experience.

Question: Are there any dangers with kuṇḍalinī awakening? It seems to be an overwhelming experience.

Gurudev: I think overwhelming is probably the right word. It is about release, or letting go, and there may be a small percentage of people whom it makes truly crazy.

But, as Baba said, the *śakti* is wise. If you allow yourself to surrender to the process and have faith, the śakti will guide you in the right way. Life then becomes full, complete. As such, there are no dangers.

Danger arises when people mix kuṇḍalinī, drugs, and other things, to experiment. If you do that, you're playing with fire. You are doing something that is not natural. That can become dangerous.

Many of the people who do go over the edge are those who have already been on the edge. To flush out that tendency, the kuṇḍalinī may push them totally over. Then they can rebuild themselves anew. The mind becomes stronger.

When I was about eight or nine years old, an American man came to Ganeshpuri. He was a little bit funny in the mind. Baba instructed him, "Don't meditate. Just do mantra repetition."

So we, the little kids, were given the job of sitting in a line along the back wall, and he had the job of walking back and forth, chanting *Śrī Rām Jai Rām*. He would chant, and we would chant. Sometimes we thought it was a punishment for us because we had to sit there for one or two hours doing this with him. He needed the chanting just to calm down.

DON'T LET YOUR MIND TRICK YOU

Question: Sometimes I'm not sure if I'm getting what I should out of your talks and the chants and the other practices. Is there a way to maximize what I'm getting?

Gurudev: It's when you get caught in "I should be doing this to get the maximum out of it" that problems sometimes arise. It is better to allow yourself to sit and participate without saying, "I should feel this" or "I shouldn't feel this" or "I should think this or not think this."

Baba used to tell a very simple story about a seeker who went to the Guru and said, "Give me initiation."

The Guru agreed and said, "Okay, here is a mantra. Now meditate." And he added, "But never think of a monkey when you meditate."

The seeker thought, "Why? I never think of monkeys. Why would I think of a monkey when I meditate?"

So he went back home and he sat. And the first thing that came to mind was a monkey. He changed directions. He changed places. He changed postures. But all he could do was think of a monkey.

He ran back to the Guru and said, "I never thought of a monkey before. But now that you've given me initiation, I can't think of the mantra. I can only think of a monkey!"

Just by doing it and by participating fully, you will get better at it. The value of what you are getting will start to grow. But if you tell yourself, "I want to make sure that in this twenty-four hours we spend together I get the maximum benefit out of everything," then your own mind will trick you. When you leave for home, you'll be asking yourself, "Did I get the maximum benefit or didn't I?" You'll start evaluating. Whereas if you just come, participate, and then return home, you'll be happy.

You see my point? Just enjoy. However much of yourself is able to participate, allow it to participate. It might be the whole thing, it might be ninety percent, it might be fifty percent. Whatever amount is fine.

Question: I feel locked into habitual experience in thought and action. What produces the shift toward spontaneity?

Gurudev: Most human beings operate from fear. However, when there is some understanding within, you realize, "What is the use of fear? It does nothing except limit me. What is to happen will happen anyway. So let me just live life and enjoy." The Sufis use the example of how animals live. Animals don't worry about tomorrow, about what to do or what will happen. They just live life in the moment and enjoy.

Ram Das teaches, "Be here now." This means living life in the moment, keeping the mind present. If you can train the mind to be in the moment and enjoy, then spontaneity can be realized. It is a process to be worked on.

Question: When you were talking before, you said to get rid of useless thoughts. But then you said, "Use your mind, use your brain." Can you explain that? Use your brain but not the useless thoughts?

Gurudev: I think you answered your own question.

Everybody thinks. There is no one who doesn't think. A dog thinks too. I'm sure a horse thinks.

I was saying that we all have a brain, and now science is finding that the less we use our brain, the more it dies. And the more it dies, the greater the chances of all these various sicknesses. So we want to use the brain to do better things.

We grew up with respect for our elders. We had fear of our elders. So out of love and respect for our elders, we used our brain to do good things. We at least attempted to do good deeds. However, the children of today don't have that fear of their elders. So they just do anything. And that filters down through society.

What we want is, as the *Vedas* say, "O my mind, have noble thoughts."

For example, you think, "I want to repeat the mantra." But you can't sit for twenty-four hours a day and repeat *Oṁ Namaḥ*

Śivāya, Oṁ Namaḥ Śivāya, Oṁ Namaḥ Śivāya. There are other things that have to take place. However, now thanks to the iPod and CD, you can have the mantra playing in the background, with the volume set at around 10. You can still hear it, and at the same time, you can go about doing whatever needs to be done.

You've heard me talk about people who watch thriller movies and then say their sleep that night is disturbed. Who asked them to watch that movie? Who asked them to scare themselves? They don't need to do that.

You can read something uplifting before you go to bed. Then you sleep well. In the morning, you wake up feeling good. And you do good things.

Ultimately, you aim for cessation of thought. But until you get to the full cessation of thought, do wise things.

This can be a constant struggle. It's difficult to be good. But we all have to make the effort to be good.

Question: I work with many people who have dementia, and I worry I'll become demented and forget my mantra. If that happens, will I still be okay as long as I don't have thoughts?

Gurudev: I think while you are still free of dementia—and of all the conditions that can come with aging—you can work really hard so every part of your body becomes filled with the mantra.

Baba often said that every cell, every pore, of the body should become filled with the mantra. So in anticipation of possible dementia, you practice that now.

I've read over the years that using more parts of the brain—whether it's through learning a language or doing different things—is associated with keeping the brain alive. If you use less of the brain, it is more likely that the brain becomes dead. So you have to find things you can do, including things you may never have done before, to keep those parts of the brain alive. Also, today many people are not aware of the effect food and other aspects of their lifestyle have on the aging process.

So chant!

A GOLDEN VESSEL

Question: Could you speak about the hazards of meditating too many hours a day?

Gurudev: I've always warned against over meditating. One thinks, "I should just meditate." But Baba didn't prescribe that. He said too much meditation consumes the fluids of the body. The scriptures prescribe many other things—study, repetition of the mantra, japa—to complement meditation.

If you look at Baba's own schedule during his sādhanā, you'll find he had an early morning meditation. Then he had a break. Then he had a mid-morning meditation. Then he had a break. Then he had a late afternoon meditation. Then he had a break. Then he had an evening meditation, around sunset. Then he had a break. And again he had one more meditation before going to sleep. So it wasn't constant, non-stop meditation. His meditation was spread out during the day, along with study, japa, walking, and some interactions with people.

The main thing the sages say is that the mind and the body aren't strong enough for so much meditation. We generate a lot of energy within ourselves as we meditate. The analogy often used is of tiger's milk and a golden vessel. Tiger's milk is said to be such that one needs a gold vessel to carry it. Whenever I mention this, I tell people, "If you're not sure, you can always get some tiger's milk and see."

The idea is that the body is a vessel. We've done so much with it that it takes a long time to cleanse and purify it so when we meditate, it can digest and hold the energy of meditation. We need to prepare and purify the physical body, and also the other bodies within it, to avoid the pitfalls of too much meditation.

Question: Is there a particular time of day that is better to do japa or repeat the mantra?

Gurudev: I think before going to bed is a great time because then the mind is filled with the mantra. And the other time is early in the morning when you first wake up.

Question: I remember reading that during his sādhanā, Baba meditated twelve to fourteen hours a day for nine years. How does that compare?

Gurudev: You have to realize that he had done twenty-five years of seeking and searching before he got to those nine years. Baba also talked about eating accordingly to make sure the body is prepared. Cashews, ghee, pistachios, and raisins are some of the foods that give us strength for meditation. We use these in our kitchen.

Around Baba, when somebody had a strong reaction in meditation, a kriyā, they would stuff a banana into that person's mouth. If one person couldn't easily handle it, two people would hold down the person having the kriyā. Sometimes it was just a little person, but even two big people had trouble holding that little person down. That's how much energy the person would have.

I don't think we fully understand śakti. I mean, we talk about it. We say what we think it is. But when śakti is raw, as we saw sometimes around Baba, we don't realize the power it contains.

I think, as the sages advise, that it's better not to risk doing too much meditation. Because all that energy can short circuit within the body. We've seen that over the years. A person "loses it" because his system can't handle it.

You ask why? A simple example is taking something made to work in the United States on 110 volts of electricity. If you put 440 volts through it, that's four times what it can handle. It's going to blow.

Question: In our world full of noise and confusion, how do I focus?

Gurudev: Our world is noisy for sure. Yesterday as we were walking here, after we'd spent a few minutes in the cottage, I said, "It's so quiet."

I think those of us who enjoy—or have learned to enjoy—silence can create silence, at least in our own spaces. We learn to turn off things that make noise. Because everything makes noise, including ourselves. The whole practice of meditation to me is learning to enjoy silence.

We play music. And at some point, we want even the music to stop. Like last night after the chant, there was a stillness. We learn to enjoy that stillness. If we're used to noise, then we're dying to make noise. We have to hold ourselves back and say, "Be still. Be quiet."

Focus is a great exercise. Over the years, we teach ourselves how to focus. Baba's experience was about focus. He put forth great effort to get to that place.

THE LIGHT SHINES THROUGH

Question: Baba talked a lot about the blue pearl. Could you explain more about it?

Gurudev: The blue pearl was what Baba experienced in his own meditation as the final goal. He used to say his experience of the Self within each one of us was a blue pearl.

The sages talk about the subtle bodies, or energy bodies, within us as light. Tukārām Mahārāj said he experienced red, white, black, yellow, and different colors. Depending on a person's inner state, you will see different colors emanate from him or her. Modern people call it an aura.

Baba used to say that whenever he saw somebody approaching him, he first saw light. He didn't see the individual, all he saw was light. For him, that was the light of the Self, which he called the blue pearl.

He said that when he was going through his process of meditation, he sometimes saw the blue pearl coming and going. As he became established in his experience of meditation, that blue light became steady.

I don't think you can read about the blue pearl in too many places other than Baba's books. That's why I say that it was his experience. Of course, after he wrote about it, many people talked about it.

Question: So is the blue pearl something we can achieve?

Gurudev: You can get to a place where you see the light of Consciousness. How you see it may be the same as someone else, or it may be different.

Within this physical body are the subtle body, causal body, and supra-causal body. They are all bodies of light, or energy bodies. When you don't meditate, you become denser. You put more covering over the light bodies. When you begin to meditate, you cleanse and purify the various bodies. Then the light shines through.

Therefore, it's often said our face is a reflection of how we are inside. The purer you become within, the brighter your face is. That brightness is not because of anything other than the light shining within you. And for that you do living yoga.

Question: I want to ask about an experience I don't understand. A few years ago, I had a meditation in which Baba Muktānanda placed a dagger in my third eye, which exploded in my head and I saw three colors: red, white, and blue. They were like jewels. I've always wondered what the colors meant.

Gurudev: In one of his poems, Tukārām Mahārāj calls these the colors of Consciousness. He says red, white, and black; he doesn't call it blue. He says these are the lights of Consciousness within.

When each of the different chakras is opened, a light is emitted. Along with the light comes a color. Tukārām talks of red, white, and black as associated with the *ājñā* chakra, what you call the third eye.

Vedānta speaks of colors as associated with the different bodies: physical, subtle, and causal. Each has its own color.

As you meditate, you see different lights and colors. I always say these are teasers to let you know something is happening, that the process is going on. This way, the love for the practices is maintained. The desire to continue is strengthened. These kinds of experiences whet the appetite for more.

THE MANTRA REDEEMS

Question: I have been practicing *Oṁ Namaḥ Śivāya*, and today you mentioned *Haṁsa*. I started to do it, but I was kind of battling with it. Could you please put some light on that?

Gurudev: You're not the only one. So thank you for that. Everybody has this issue when they've done *Oṁ Namaḥ Śivāya*, or some mantra, for a period of time. They wonder, "How do I do *Haṁsa* when my mind automatically goes to *Oṁ Namaḥ Śivāya*?"

As you sit for meditation every day, you begin to become aware of the full breathing process. We breathe, but it's very rare that we find ourselves taking a full, deep breath, down to the abdomen, and a full exhalation up from the abdomen.

First allow yourself to become aware of the inhalation and exhalation. When you find you are able to inhale and exhale from the abdomen, then along with that breath, do *Haṁ* and *Sa*.

The philosophy of Kashmir Shaivism explains that this is the sound the breath makes as it goes in and goes out. Up to a certain point, you repeat *Haṁ* and *Sa*. Then you find that you become quiet. Sometimes you will hear yourself doing the mantra. But you aren't actually doing it. It is happening.

Then the question arises, "What do I do with *Oṁ Namaḥ Śivāya*?"

As you go about your daily activities, without being aware of your breathing, without trying to go into meditation, repeat *Oṁ Namaḥ Śivāya*. Remind yourself in one way or another that all of this is a reflection of Consciousness.

How can you do that? You can't say, "Reflection, reflection, reflection, reflection, reflection, reflection." So you say *Oṁ Namaḥ Śivāya*. And that reminds you it's a reflection. It reminds you to smile. It reminds you to laugh. It reminds you to simply sit back and enjoy.

You use the mantra *Haṁsa* as a means of concentration, of focus. And you use *Oṁ Namaḥ Śivāya* as a reminder.

Question: If a person repeats a mantra, either consciously or unconsciously, with the wrong pronunciation, can that person kill somebody else or himself because of the power of the mantra?

Gurudev: You won't kill yourself with the power of mantra. Mantra means "that which redeems." When you do it with a positive understanding, it helps you and uplifts you.

There are people who use mantras to do bad things. Yet if at the same time you repeat a mantra that protects you, you won't be hurt by that other person. I've always found that the person who chooses the positive route wins.

ALL THIS IS A REFLECTION

Question: Can you speak about ways of staying connected to this living yoga at times when the mind needs to be focused on practical, worldly things?

Gurudev: The philosophy of Shaivism talks about a practice called *ābhāsavāda*. It means seeing everything as a reflection.

Let's begin with the simple theory of reflection. There is a mirror. Objects are reflected in the mirror. Now, both are real—the reflection and the objects. Anything that happens to the objects affects those objects. Yet nothing happens to the mirror. The mirror is independent, right?

What you are asking me is "How should I perceive this big reflection?"

Apply the same concept as you go into the world. All you see there is nothing but a reflection of universal Consciousness. Not every object is aware of the fact that it is a reflection. Moreover, there is no mirror there between you and the reflection to remind you that all this is a reflection. You have to know.

If you go out into the world with the understanding that all of this is a reflection of that one Consciousness, your whole attitude in dealing with everybody changes.

It is okay to mentally say, "Everything is a reflection." But there is a reality you have to deal with. You can't drive behind a car and say, "It's a reflection, so I won't bump into it." That's not true. You're going to bump into it. But at the same time, remember it's simply a reflection.

I brought Baba's book with me. And I just looked at the title: *Reflections of the Self.*

He wants us to understand how long a reflection is good for. As long as you stand in front of a mirror, there is a reflection. The moment you move away from the mirror, there is no reflection. As long as the body is here, there is a reflection. The moment the body passes, there is no more reflection. It's gone.

Often I ask myself, "How do sages who live in the experience of the Self at all times deal with this world?"

They are aware that everything is Consciousness, yet they

have to deal with us. I think they don't allow themselves to move away from the experience of oneness, of bigness, of awareness, or whatever you want to call it. They remain expanded. We contract. Our contraction comes about because of fear, because of limitedness.

So the question you want to ask is "How do I get rid of this limitedness?" Because, as Baba said, a human being has the potential, the power, to be anything. We can be good, we can be bad. We can do good, we can do bad. We limit ourselves by immediately telling ourselves, "No, it's not possible. I can't do that."

I think when you are dealing with the world, rather than think something can't be done, you have to look at it the other way. Think of what is possible, what can be done. The only question is how.

It's all about managing people's perceptions. Think of what the media does. It manages your perception. All of sudden, a million people all over the world have read the same news. And a million people have the same thought: "Oh my God!"

I think about what Baba did in his time. He got so many people to chant. He got so many people to meditate. Historically, there have been places, such as Pandharpur or Alandi, where great crowds of people gather to chant. Okay, it's hot, it's dusty, it's dirty. It's all of that. But if you can rise above that, there is the collective experience.

In your own workplaces, see if you can create an environment of awareness, of Consciousness. Many business places, companies, and factories in India gather their workers to chant. They do āratī. Recently, a man brought a group of his coworkers here so they could experience something other than what they normally experience. One lady liked it, and she brought her husband and parents.

Because what we do here is so different, I think we get scared. We wonder, "What should I tell people?"

When I go to a grocery store, sometimes there's a child who has the courage to say, "Mommy, what's a man doing in a skirt?" She goes, "Shh!"

The child continues to watch me, and as we meet in different aisles, continues to wonder, "What is that man doing in a skirt?"

All I can do is smile because I know the mother is afraid I might convert the child into who I am. Of course, I have a dress that makes me obvious. But you can bring awareness into your workplace in other ways. Realize that, just as you were ignorant some years ago, your colleagues, friends, and family might be like that now.

It's not about coming in and saying, "Okay, everything is God! Everything is Consciousness." That will immediately put them off.

Think of ways to share this teaching. Let them know you're trying to live a better life. You're trying to act consciously. You're trying to watch your thoughts. Many people don't even know they can be aware of their thoughts. Some think, "I have thoughts. What can I do about it?" However, we can have better thoughts.

So the question arises: "How do I improve the quality of my thoughts?"

Baba said, "Read good books. Listen to good music. Keep good company." And then? Well, start with that. Of course, they'll ask, "What should I read?" So be ready with what you want to give them to read.

All of these are props. They begin the conversation. Of course, for you they serve as reminders that this is a reflection. Because it is possible in the moment to forget.

All of us have to find ways to remember the teachings. Brahmānanda Mahārājji used to do this. Baba used to do this. He always carried a pocket version of the *Bhagavad Gītā*, or another scripture. That way, when you're sitting idly, instead of having wasteful thoughts, you can open the book.

I remember when we were with Mahārājji in 1995, in Calcutta. Early in the morning, we all gathered on the lawn for breakfast. He was seated on his chair, reading his small *Bhagavad Gītā*. I thought, "He's been a monk for fifty or sixty years. He's got the whole thing backwards and forwards. He knows all the verses. He knows everything." So I said, "Let's ask him why he is reading this at eight o'clock in the morning." Normally one would want to read the newspaper, to know the latest gossip. So we asked him.

He said, "I am Arjuna. And this is Kṛṣṇa speaking to me." Over the sixty years, somewhere along the line, he realized Arjuna is not somebody else. The teachings aren't just for preaching or sharing, they are what we have to learn. Take away the distinction that this is a conversation between Arjuna and Kṛṣṇa on the battlefield. No, this is my battlefield. I am Arjuna. And Kṛṣṇa is speaking to me. These teachings are for me.

When we read Baba's books, we think, "Wow, Baba said such great things." But then we read *Reflections of the Self* and see that he says, "Wash your face and hands. Whatever food you receive, whether tasty or dry, eat it only after purifying your mind. Don't be tantalized by delicious food. If you are given dry food, don't be angry."

You might say, "Well, of course, I'll wash my face and hands." But what you really have to remember is "If you are given dry food, don't be angry."

Sometimes when you're on an airplane, the flight attendant serves you something you can't eat. In that moment, realize this is all the person can do. Simply because you would be able to do more, don't think he or she is able to do more. That reflection can only do that much. This is the capacity of that reflection. We want to force our reflection upon that reflection. It's not possible.

To me, this is what living yoga is about. It's about living the teachings, the principles, constantly. Put yourself in the other person's shoes and think, "What would I have done?" Once in a while, a flight attendant who finds out we're vegetarians will be creative and say, "I'll be back." Someone else will just say, "Did you order it beforehand?" and won't get us anything.

Usually we don't want anything anyway because we have come prepared. But it's fun to see how this person will behave.

Whenever somebody is not nice, or is mean, it's a good lesson. We can remind ourselves, "This is how I don't want to be when I am in a situation like this." Of course, that means we also say to ourselves, "How *do* I want to be?"

In all our dealings in the world, we simply ask, "How would I like to be dealt with?" And then deal with others accordingly.

Question: If you are confused, how do you know you're making the right decision?

Gurudev: I have a question. When I ask myself the question, an answer comes. The answer comes softly, gently. I listen to that answer. I am aware that my question has been answered.

But suppose instead of following that very first response, I go and get a few opinions. A dozen people give me a dozen opinions. Then I am confused! I may have a dozen opinions, but I've forgotten that first response.

We as seekers have to learn to trust that first response. It comes from a place of truth, of Consciousness.

That doesn't mean everything will work out perfectly as we go along. But we will arrive at our destination. The reason those obstacles come is because Consciousness wants to see how determined we are to get to our goal. Will a distraction take us away from our goal or will we keep going no matter what happens?

If I am coming from Mexico City to here, I can get lost. There could be a traffic jam. The road could be closed. Last time we came, we had four flat tires. Every time we had to look for a place to repair the tire. Now, I can say, "Well, God didn't really want me to go there." Or I can say, "God wanted to see how much I really wanted to get there."

I can say to myself, "These are just little things happening on the way. They're going to happen to someone, so today it's me." And I can keep going.

This is what focus teaches us. We don't get distracted by all these things.

Nor do we dig too deep and say, "What is God trying to teach me here?"

I ran into a pothole, so I had a flat tire. Or I didn't do my homework to find out the road was being repaired. We become wise.

The question is, "What is my goal?" That is what I have to become clear about. When I am clear about my destination, I have to stay focused and get there. That is the clarity each one of us must maintain.

WE ARE ALL LIGHT

Question: When I meditate I see a blue light, and then I disappear. I don't know if it's been five minutes or an hour; there's no awareness. Is that a lower form of samādhi? And what is the next step?

Gurudev: Often people see blue light in different forms. As Baba said, that blue light is the light of Consciousness. He suggested you to get to a place where that blue light remains steady in your experience.

Question: In my waking experience?

Gurudev: In all three states of waking, dream, and deep sleep. And of course in the state in which you experience the Self.

Baba's experience was that all of us are light. Therefore, we need to see that light.

Right now we experience ourselves and everything else in its gross, physical form. We don't see the light. Once in a while we get a glimpse of it. So we must bring ourselves to a deeper place within, where we always see the light.

The other day during meditation, someone fell off her chair. Everybody was concerned for a few moments, but she was fine. When I met her later, she told me she was actually the most relaxed she's ever been when it happened.

Through meditation, we can all come to that place within. Being relaxed means being at ease with ourselves. Even though we are living with ourselves at all times, most of us don't realize we aren't at ease.

How does a yogi get to that state? When we go to a place of quiet within, I think it is because we have accepted ourselves and let go of all judgments. Baba's teaching that we are all light is not about going to a place of void or emptiness. We go to a place you could call love or bliss.

Sometimes I wonder if it's necessary to give it a label. It's just a wonderful place in which these different experiences happen. In our limited state, we want to say, "Is this love? Is this joy? Is this bliss? Is this where the mind dissolves?" The scriptures say, "When salt mixes in water, what is salt and what is water? They have become one." So if I also become like that, it doesn't matter what happens to me. What matters is that I have dissolved.

Question: Totally disappear?

Gurudev: To some people, that's a scary thought because they have their identities. And in the place you go to, there is no identity. There's just an expanded state of Consciousness.

THE POINT OF MEDITATION

Question: So you say we get to this place of stillness. Is there any point to that?

Gurudev: Until you have experienced stillness and quietude, you wonder what it will be like.

Being still doesn't mean the world stops. The world continues. But the mind isn't filled with so many thoughts.

We grew up in the ashram, and we were taught over and over again to have as few thoughts as possible. Now I realize that so many people the world over have millions of thoughts.

I travel a lot, and I put my head on many pillows in different beds. One can feel that some pillows have a lot of thoughts. When I become aware of this, I move the pillow. And I think, "How does this individual live with so many thoughts?"

Before you even get to a place where there are no thoughts, you have to reduce, reduce, reduce, reduce, reduce.

Now you have random thoughts, thoughts with no purpose. You may wonder, "Why am I having these thoughts?"

So you go through a process of elimination. First you eliminate all erratic thoughts. You eliminate useless thoughts.

One day you come to a place of very few thoughts. And those few thoughts are useful thoughts. They are focused thoughts. As Baba would say, instead of being the servant of your mind, your mind becomes your servant.

Some people are afraid of quiet. They tell me that too much quiet is not good. You can read advertisements selling CDs for people who live in Manhattan and aren't used to silence all the time. When they go to the country, they have to take a CD of the city noise so they can sleep at night.

Baba used to tell a story about a florist and a fisherman who are friends. The florist invites the fisherman to his house to spend the day. He puts out beautiful, fragrant flowers for the fisherman to enjoy.

The fisherman comes. He's not at ease. He lies down, but he can't go to sleep. He gets a headache. So he goes to the florist and says, "You know, friend, you put out these beautiful flowers, but they are giving me a headache."

In India a fisherman has a basket covered with a gunnysack, and it has a strong smell of fish. The florist realizes his friend is used to that fish smell. So he brings him his basket and says, "Here, sleep with this next to you." The fisherman takes a nice, deep breath and says, "Good!" And he falls asleep.

Therefore Baba would say, "We all get used to our fragrance." You may not know what your fragrance is, but it is the fragrance of the mental processes you are used to. If you have a disturbed mind, you're used to your disturbed mind. You don't know what a quiet mind is. You don't know what it's like to be happy. You don't know what it's like to be peaceful. You have to allow yourself to enjoy a different fragrance.

Those of us who spent time around Baba noticed a certain fragrance that came with him. Sometimes you smelled it even before he came into the room. Over the years, many people have said it was heena, a scented oil he applied. But I came to the realization it had nothing to do with that oil. It was a fragrance he had.

I believe all of us develop a fragrance within. Until you've had that experience, you cannot understand what it is. Once you have realized a certain fragrance—whether it is bliss or peace or quiet—you don't want to live without it.

I have found in my years of travel that all successful people meditate. They don't call it meditation, because they are thinking. But each one gets up early and sits on a chair for an hour. If you ask these people what they are doing, they say, "Planning for the day." But I think they are meditating, they are focusing their thoughts.

Unsuccessful people just get out of bed and run. They don't make anything out of life because they haven't gathered their thoughts. They just run from thought to thought to thought.

So meditation is a process of elimination. You learn slowly what not to keep. You keep only that which is useful and necessary, and become free of the rest. That is the point.

PRACTICE HAS TO BE ALIVE

Question: Is it most auspicious to chant the *Guru Gītā* in the morning? I'm not sure if it's okay to chant it in the evening.

Gurudev: It depends upon your lifestyle and your work schedule. If your schedule allows you to do it in the morning, that is the best time.

When you chant in a group, it takes forty to forty-five minutes. But if you do it on your own, you can do it in twenty minutes. So it doesn't take that long.

I have seen over the years that the best time for any practice is early morning. No other time is quite like four o'clock to six or six thirty. There's something special about nature at that time.

Once the sun has risen, the vehicles have started moving and everybody is going. It's hard to say, "Now I'm going to put in my earplugs and try to sit quietly." It's not quite the same. By then nature also has fully blossomed.

It is all a matter of adjustment. If it is easier for you, you can do your practice when you come back from work. Wash up. Take that hour, hour and a half, or two hours to practice. Then go to sleep.

Question: What about the location?

Gurudev: Despite what you read in the *Guru Gītā*, I don't think it's a sin to chant it anywhere. What the sage is trying to tell you is to find a place, to find a practice. To do it, do it, do it!

They know if they scare you with sin, then you will do it. But if you read with understanding, you realize there is no such thing. It's just that to scare you into doing the practice at a particular time and place every day, this three-letter word has crept in. The worst thing about it is that you feel bad. And there's no sin worse than that.

Hopefully all of us are living the teachings, the practices, the knowledge, and all that has been imparted to us. Making that a part of our life is what is most important.

I always share that you can choose one practice, one teaching, you like. You tell yourself, "Okay, I can do this." That is better than nothing. In fact, I would say that's wonderful because at least there's one teaching you can say you have taken, totally imbibed, practiced, and made your own. It has become real for you. Simply follow that. In your own time, when you feel ready, you will pick up something else.

For example, take Baba's message "Meditate on yourself, honor yourself, worship yourself, God dwells within you as you." You can choose any part: meditate, honor, worship, God dwells within you as you. If it is honor, you can say, "I'll just remember to honor, I'll just remember to honor, I'll just remember to honor." Wherever you go, no matter what happens, you remember to be honorable. It becomes part of you. Whether you are awake or dreaming or sleeping, or no matter what you are doing, that teaching cannot be separated from you.

I think that's when the practice, the teaching, the knowledge has become alive. Until then it's only in books.

When you go back home, look through your books. I tell people, borrow a book. Because you don't usually read the same book twice. And don't highlight or mark in books. If something appeals to you, keep a notebook and write it there. You don't need to write too many details. I don't think that's important. What is important is the teaching.

You may forget in ten years what book you read, or what sage it was, but you will always have your own notebook. You will have a record of the teaching that illuminated itself inside you. When you read it again ten years later, it will illuminate even more because you will have walked that much farther on the path.

People like to look at yearbooks. But your own notebook is the best yearbook. In it, there is nothing good, nothing bad. There is nothing right, there is nothing wrong. There is just where you are today, where you were five years ago, where you were ten years ago. Some things will bring a smile when you reread them because you'll have memories of what happened then. And you'll realize within yourself, "I have moved along." Within us is a lot of memory—more memory than a computer has. I'm sure you are amazed sometimes at how much we remember. God has given us infinite terabytes.

Question: When you read the translation of the *Guru Gītā*, there's some pretty weird stuff about sitting on different things, facing different directions. Are we meant to take it literally?

Gurudev: Yes, the seating directions and so on do have literal meanings. But you need to be very committed, very intent on doing it, if you want to see results.

For example, the *Guru Gītā* says facing north is for peace, and facing west is for wealth. So you sit and say to yourself, "I am sitting on this *āsana*, facing north to acquire peace." As with everything in life, intensity must be there. If you just sit there with the book, facing north, not really into it, then nothing much may happen.

The ritualistic part of the *Vedas* is filled with these kinds of practices: the direction to face, the deity to please, the mantras to use. The Brahmin priests can look at someone's astrological chart and prescribe what that individual can do to please the relevant deity.

The way I look at it, there is the one energy of God, but different subdivisions of that energy perform various functions to enable the universe to work. The deities are different energies, performing these different jobs.

PERSONAL DAILY PRACTICE

Question: Lavarji told me to do *sandhyā*. But I've never done it. I thought I'd just do what Baba told us to do: the mantra, meditation, kirtan. Am I being stubborn? Is that wrong?

Gurudev: Lavarji is a priest. He joins us for a couple of months. Then he goes away. He comes, and he goes. Every morning he chants mantras in addition to those he does here in front of all of us. And when he meets an individual, he tries to share his knowledge with that person. I think there is nothing wrong in listening to what he wants to share, and then asking yourself, "How can I apply this to the teachings my Guru has given me?"

The word *sandhyā* means dawn and dusk. In other words, the junctures of the day. Some practices have to be done at those times.

Baba has given us these practices. The question to ask ourselves is "How much do I really do?"

Some people come to the ashram and say, "Well, I have to go home and rest now."

I ask them why.

They say, "Here I have to get up early. I do a lot throughout the day. Then I go to bed and wake up early again the next day. At home I can sleep in. At home I can sleep whenever I want."

These are people who have been on the path for twenty, thirty years. My thought is "Something is wrong somewhere."

What is important is that you find the time—no matter how busy, no matter how occupied you are—to do your practice. Create a schedule. Don't just do it when you come to the ashram. Don't just do it when you come together as a community or as a group of friends.

We have people here who, knowing the āratī begins at 6:30 a.m., get up at 6:25. They have a quick brush, throw on a little water, and show up in the temple. That is not the idea.

The idea is that you get up early in the ashram and do whatever daily practice you have created at home. That is your individual practice. When you come into the temple, you do a group practice with everybody. That's a bonus, in addition to whatever individual practices you do.

The question to ask yourself is "What have I created as my own personal daily practice?" It could be *Haṁsa, Oṁ Namaḥ Śivāya,* kirtan, the *Guru Gītā.* Then you ask, "How was I five years ago? How am I today?"

I don't think we can have an exam for sādhanā. You can say, "I'm very good." But if your friends tell you otherwise, then you can't just say they are wrong in how they judge you. When we feel judged, it is natural to think others shouldn't judge us. But in this case, you have to ask yourself, "What do I do now? How do I improve? How do I get better? How do I evolve?"

There are a lot of teachings out there. The question is how much of that knowledge do you actually apply on a daily basis in your life? How much do you actually use?

In his books, Baba talks about how a person can be a great scholar. A person can have a lot of knowledge, a lot of information. But that does not necessarily mean he knows it.

The example I give is of a CD or a video. That CD contains a lot of information, but that doesn't mean the CD player has imbibed it. All of us can read books, can quote from books, but how much do we really know? Do the teachings really resonate within us? That is the question.

Coming together in satsaṅg whenever you can helps make this apparent. When you are in a group of like-minded people, and you each share with and check each other, you see how much you have really understood of all that has been taught and all that you have read.

WHERE THE SOUL GOES

Question: Since I was a child, I've been curious about where we go when we die. I'm still curious. Is it *siddha loka*?

Gurudev: I'm sure everybody is curious.

A lady lost her ninety-three-year-old husband today. So we called to talk to her this afternoon.

She said to me, "Wherever he is, may he be well."

In *Play of Consciousness*, Baba talks about different planes of existence, which we call lokas, where the soul goes after death. The eighth chapter of the *Bhagavad Gītā* talks about the whole process of death. It teaches us how to die, so I will begin with that.

Most people don't know there are four ways for the soul to leave the body. You might know that when some people die, they excrete. Somebody mentioned thinking these people are getting rid of dirt from the body. But actually the soul has left through the anus. It is considered the worst form of death. Such a person has not lived a good life or performed good actions.

Another way is through the mouth. In that case, the mouth will be open as the soul leaves the body. The third way is through the eyes.

The fourth way is through the sahasrāra, at the top of the head. Only a yogi leaves this way. The body has five types of *prāṇa*, and it takes the yogi approximately twenty to thirty minutes to gather all his prāṇa and then leave through the sahasrāra.

When somebody dies, usually the first question I ask is "How did he die? Did he suffer or did he just go?"

Sometimes people say, "Well, he had breathing issues. Or he had pain, or this and that." Some people go in their sleep. Others have a massive heart attack. Of course, you can have a heart attack, and then the doctors try to bring you back. But the best thing, as Baba used to say, is that if you think you are a yogi, then on your deathbed you prove to the world how good a yogi you are.

Within the physical body is a subtle body with nineteen

limbs. The subtle body is made of light, and when the soul leaves, it travels in that body.

According to our philosophy, where we go after death depends on how we have lived upon Earth. Earth is the one place where we can work out karma. If you have created good karma, you go to one of the planes Baba talked about. For a period of time, the soul, or subtle body, lives there and enjoys the pleasures of that world. When the good karma you have created is finished, once again the soul comes back onto this Earth in a physical form.

It is up to us what we do with this life. I always think I can't really worry about death or what will happen to me after death. I have to be good while I live my life. If I want the time that I leave the body to be good, and my life after I leave this body to be good, I have to be good all the time.

My theory is that good actions must become constant. All thoughts must be good. All speech must be good. And I want to clarify that I don't mean superficially good. Sometimes we say, "Oh wow, that was good!" No, let it be good with depth, really good. We must feel, think, and do good not because we have to, but because it comes naturally.

GRACE IS ALWAYS THERE

Question: We can do a lot of practices, but I'd like to hear more about Guru's grace.

Gurudev: All of these practices prepare us to tap into grace.

Grace is like the sunlight. It is always there. But right now it looks like there is no sun. It's dark. But that is simply a dark cloud over the sun. In a few moments, the cloud will be gone and the sun will shine again.

In the same way, our mind is like a dark cloud. All our doubts, all our negativities, are like clouds that cover the sun. Yoga, all the practices, everything we do here, is to make sure the clouds always go quickly.

You may feel grace is not there. But I feel grace is always there. All we have to do is connect with it.

This recorder is fifty percent charged. By the end of the day, it will be zero percent charged. At ten percent, it will remind me that I have to charge it. If I'm smart, I will plug it in at that point and recharge it. Then it will be ready to use again in two hours.

In the same way, every day we use our internal battery. By the end of the day, it is discharged. One way we recharge it is by sleeping. The second way is to get up and do some chanting and meditation. That charges your whole self.

Every day that you don't do your spiritual practices, your battery discharges. And you wonder why. But you just have to plug in. You make sure you plug in every day. Then you remain connected, you remain charged.

This is why we talk about the Guru's grace. When we stay connected to grace, we feel the Guru is always with us.

Driving here, we could see Montserrat. Whoever drives this way receives the darśan of the mountain. He feels connected to grace just by seeing the mountain.

If you go to old places around Europe, you find that the tallest building was always the church. No matter where you were, you could see its steeple. You could remain connected to God by looking at it. Now many buildings are taller than the church, so we must make an extra effort to go to where the temple of God is.

In the same way, when you find your means or technique of connecting with grace, use it.

Your means might be to carry your photos or music. Whenever you forget, all you do is turn on your music, and in a moment you are there.

Earlier, I played Baba's talk just for two minutes. You hear him, and in a moment you are in his presence. Whatever else is going on in your mind, the Guru is present.

One day somebody who works with me was going from the ashram. He was alone in his car, and he noticed he was being followed by some bad people. Just a kilometer away, two policemen stopped him and said, "Take us in your car."

He took them with him, and they told him where to drop them.

He thought to himself, "This must be Bhagavān Nityānanda and Baba." The two policemen were protecting him, so he felt he was in the presence of the two Gurus. He felt their grace.

Grace is always there. Of course, we have to have the eyes to see it.

Many stories try to show this. For example, a man is a big devotee of God. It's raining, and a flood is coming. As the water is rising, he prays, "God, come and protect me."

A boat comes, and the captain says, "I'll take you."

The man says, "No, no, God is coming."

The water keeps rising until he's on top of his house.

A helicopter comes and they say, "We'll throw a rope. Hold on and we'll save you."

The man says, "No, no, God is coming."

Of course, the water continues to rise, and he dies and goes to heaven. He's very angry. He says, "I prayed to you, God, and you never came!"

God says, "I sent you a boat and a helicopter. What can I do if you didn't take the help?"

We sometimes get caught in what we think is God, what we

think is grace. It's there in front of us, but because it doesn't live up to our imagination, we send it away. We say, "I'll wait for my imagination of God."

We hear such a story from Bhagavān Nityānanda's life also. A woman invites him to her house for lunch.

At that time a black dog comes to her house and goes straight to the food.

She beats him and sends him away.

When she comes to Ganeshpuri some days later, she says to Bhagavān, "You never came to my house for lunch."

He says, "Do you recall that black dog you beat and pushed away?"

The Guru tries to teach us to see God in everything. Of course, we have to be able to say, "Okay, I see You."

We were in Ganeshpuri in January, and we were sitting with an old devotee of Bhagavān.

A lady came and sat with us. She said, "I'm so happy I could come for your darśan today."

The man asked, "Why?"

She said, "My nephew is sick and I've been taking care of him. This morning I wanted to come to Ganeshpuri, so I prayed to Bhagavān to take care of him."

Immediately the man asked, "Who was taking care of him before?"

She was quiet. Because her understanding had been that she was taking care of the boy, and that Bhagavān would take care of him only until she returned.

This is the kind of shift in our understanding that needs to take place.

We need to recognize that grace is always taking care. We are just an instrument doing our job. We have to become aware of grace in our life, and be grateful for its presence.

NEVER MISS A DAY

Question: The practices are like trial and error with me sometimes. I'm not focused on being aware and I just space out.

Gurudev: Take the help of whatever will remind you to be aware. It could be a picture or a symbol or another object. People keep things in their homes from their family or things that were given to them by their friends. And when they see those things, they are reminded of the ones they love.

People who came to the ashram would see the pictures of great beings on the walls and they would ask Baba, "Why do you have all these pictures around?"

He would say, "When you see their pictures, what happens? You think of what they taught."

In your home, you can create a space where you sit every day. What I find most important is to have a little altar with a lamp or a candle. You can light incense and do a little ritual, such as chanting *Jyota se Jyota*, and that inspires you to sit for meditation. Then even if you only sit for a few minutes after you chant, you will have a great meditation.

I believe it is far better to have a great five- or ten-minute meditation than to sit for one hour while your mind is wandering and filled with thoughts.

Question: How do I start my spiritual practices again if I have stopped for some time? What is the most elegant or efficient way?

Gurudev: Never let go of the daily practices. Even on the worst day, when you really don't feel like doing the practices, make yourself do them. The day you miss them once is the day they are gone.

Then you say, "Well, I missed yesterday, but that's okay, I'll start tomorrow."

But tomorrow never comes.

Never miss one day. If you can't do your practice in the morning, do it in the evening. If you can't do it in the evening, do it in the morning. But do it.

At times, I've been like that with exercise. I started, I stopped. I started, I stopped. If I missed it for one day, it could be days or months before I got back into it. I would tell myself, "Well, I'll wait for summer. Winter is too cold." But when summer came, I thought, "I'm so busy, I just don't have time."

Now, that never happened with spiritual practices. Perhaps this is because of Baba. The fear of God was there, and also the experience of joy. I always made sure I did the practices—not because I had to, but because of the joy in doing them.

Tiredness is usually the cause of the days we skip our spiritual practices. The body feels totally exhausted. Perhaps there are other reasons too. But on those days especially, we must do the practice, even if only for a few minutes.

If you have to, you can do a shortened version of what you would normally do. Or you can sit for fifteen, twenty minutes and do nothing, before you get into the practice you wish to do. Figure out for yourself what works for you.

Once you create self-discipline and make it a part of your life, it stays with you.

After bathing in the morning, I always do my *pūjā* and meditation. It comes naturally. The mind automatically goes to it. That's the advantage of a routine. When the time arrives, the mind automatically goes in that direction.

Question: When one falls and can't jump back into japa or chanting or whatever practice, what is your recommendation for getting back to that practice?

Gurudev: That is when you need to have good friends. You can call or talk to them, and they help you come back up.

Sometimes you feel lonely. You feel, "What can I do?" At that time, you can call a good friend. You don't have to say, "I fell down." You just call and talk, and you feel better.

Or you can keep a notebook, a journal. Later, when you feel down, you can look back at what you wrote. Something may strike you. You get the lift you need from what you have written.

When you reach a place of *tamas*, of darkness, you want to have things around that are uplifting. Then everything you look at tells you, "Get up! Get up! Get up!" You are left with no choice but to think, "Okay, everything I look at is telling me to uplift myself."

All of us come to this place at different times in our life. We find different techniques and methods to uplift ourselves. That's why you must be clear about what technique works for you. Sometimes it might mean getting out of the place where you are and going somewhere else altogether.

It is also important to clean your space. Get rid of all that you don't need. Only keep that which is good and uplifting. That may be books, pictures, notes, music.

You may not be aware of the subtle energies in a space. Sometimes energy becomes stagnant, and you must make it fresh again. If you have had something in the same place for a long time, move it. Clean it. Then reset it. Light lamps. Light incense. Bring in flowers.

The purpose of all this is to create a movement of energy.

A good time to do this is when you are angry. There's a lot of energy in anger that has to be released. When you clean or do other kinds of work, it's released. Instead of getting angry or doing something harmful, you do something productive.

After some hours, you're tired and wonder why you started to do all this. You laugh to yourself when you realize, "Ah, I was angry." You may not even remember why you were angry. But at least you have a clean space.

These are different things we learn to do. We constantly move and shift the energy. We have the ability to rise up. It's just that sometimes we become lazy and say, "It's not possible." So change that mantra and say, "Yes, it's possible."

Everything's okay? ¿Todo bien?

THE BEST REDEMPTION

Question: What should you do if you've done something you know isn't right or made a terrible decision? I know the first thing is, okay, resolve to not let it happen again. But still, there are all the things you've created, all the people you might have hurt. What's the best way to redeem yourself?

Gurudev: I think the fact that you've just realized what you've done is the best redemption.

If you go around and try to clarify what you've done, you only risk getting into more trouble. I mean, it gets silly if you try to go up to each and every person and say, "I am sorry, I shouldn't have done that."

Then he or she says, "What did you do?" The person doesn't even know what you are saying you're sorry for.

Of course, it depends on what the situation is. But if it's just a small thing that happened, and if you feel the other person would understand, you can explain what you've realized. Otherwise, you just trust that universal Consciousness will take care of it.

Every day, we pray in the *Evening Āratī*,

yad-akṣaraṁ padaṁ bhraṣṭaṁ
mātrā-hīnaṁ ca yad bhavet
tat sarvaṁ kṣamyatāṁ deva
prasīda parameśvara

We ask the Lord, "Please forgive me for whatever I have done that I was not aware of."

When we recite that prayer, I see some fold their hands, others close their eyes. There's an awareness that, "I've done many things today. Some I know were good. Some I know were bad. Some I don't know what they were. But I ask for Your forgiveness."

So each day, at the end of the day, when you are in the temple, or before you go to bed, just say, "Okay. Thank you. Sorry. Good night." As you do that, slowly you come to a place within yourself where you are aware that your actions, even those you unconsciously perform, have become better and better and better.

BE WHO YOU ARE

Question: I'm happy when I'm on the spiritual path. Then something gets in my way and I decide I don't want to do it anymore. Yet something inside tells me that is not the way, and I go back again. Sometimes it feels like trying to struggle through bad memories from my past life.

Gurudev: I think what you are saying is probably true or applicable for everybody. Each one has his own struggle. Whichever way you get to it—I don't want to say "by hook or by crook" because we always want to try the good way—but whichever way you get to it is fine.

Whatever you do, do it regularly. Do it daily. Don't allow the mind to control you so much by judging "I'm good" or "I'm bad."

What you need to bring about is a balance. For example, you are so passionately into your meditation, that the śakti gets roused very wildly. So find a balance whereby you're not so into it today and then not into it at all tomorrow. Break that cycle.

Question: I do meditation. I feel good about my life. And then I have the outside influences of the news of the world, and powerlessness creeps in. I take care of myself; I teach by talking to people. But is there anything else?

Gurudev: One of the conclusions I've come to, especially since 9/11, is that we, as people who are like-minded, need to do more through talking, through being fearless. We think our whole focus as yogis is inward. But one thing I love about yoga is that it teaches us how to operate from the inner to the outer. Then, wherever we go, we can bring that peace with us and share it with others.

So the question arises, have we actually made the world better? How are things different?

I think we have to get out there and do more.

It's not that nothing has come from what you're already doing, or that nothing will come from it. But the more of us who make these efforts, the greater will be the effect.

That doesn't necessarily mean becoming an activist, or becoming crazy in some way. Sometimes I cringe when people on the spiritual path use such flowery terms: "Become soft! Become gentle!" Just be who you are!

Sometimes we make ourselves so proper, and we try to appear so normal. There is an American named Krishna Das who does kirtan. We were very excited the other day because he was selected as a Grammy nominee. He always wears a t-shirt and a flannel shirt. Always.

When we heard Krishna Das was going to perform at the Grammys, we wondered if he was going to wear his signature t-shirt and flannel shirt. And that's what he wore. He didn't wear a tuxedo. He didn't wear a tie. He didn't wear a jacket. He just went as himself.

It probably took a lot of courage and chutzpah. People around him must have said, "You can't go like that. You'll look like a fool." But he had to say to himself, "This is who I am. This is how I'm going to be."

When I travel through the airport, I don't try to hide that I'm a swami. Sometimes a child will say, "Mommy, why is the man wearing a skirt?" If I hear that, I take the opportunity to smile back at the mother, to show that I'm not a weird or strange or alien creature. To show "I'm just like you, but I've chosen to do something else."

If they are close enough, I quickly say, "I'm from India. I'm a monk. I'm a swami."

They say, "Okay."

They might go home and look up what *swami* means. But at least the ignorance and fear have been lessened in the parent's mind.

As you said, we can talk to people. And we can do other things too. For example, you can hold the door open for the person behind you. You don't have to act as if you don't see that he or she is behind you. People think, "If I'm nice, they will wonder what's wrong with me." Nothing! Let them reciprocate your nicety.

Often people say, "*They* are doing it."

My question is "Who are *they*?" They're not aliens. They're not people who came from somewhere. They are simply people we have alienated from us because we haven't learned how to love them.

I was just reading a book by an American swami, who passed away. He shares a letter from a young Indian girl in Malaysia. She was getting ready to commit suicide. But she wrote to this swami and his people before attempting it. When the swami received the letter, he contacted her and her parents. I'm sure the swami felt good that he was able to stop that suicide. The girl wanted her letter shared so it could help other people who are feeling the same thing. I think oftentimes we don't know how to reach out when we are in trouble ourselves. And we don't know what to do to help a person who is in trouble.

In society today, we have put on so many layers. At some point, certain people get fed up and snap. This anger is what we've been seeing on the news in the last few weeks. When we were in California, we saw it again. Often they shoot themselves at the end, and you realize their anger and frustration are not at something out there. Their frustration is within themselves.

I always feel that gatherings like this satsaṅg need to happen more often. People can come, listen, think, and keep coming back. It's when one stays alone at home, and doesn't have somebody else to go to, that one conjures up ideas and thoughts and visions.

These days, many people don't have places where they feel they can go. In India, in my childhood, if you knew somebody who lived in your neighborhood was a friend and a good person, you would go to such a person. You knew you could hang out with him and get rid of any frustration. You might not necessarily know you were frustrated, but yet you would go. You'd think, "He's wise enough because he's a little bit older." He didn't know why you came, but he'd think, "Something's a little tweaked here." So you talked. When you got home, you had a better sense of how you could handle things.

My parents too welcomed visitors. In the early days, my mother would have a towel and a change of clothes available. In India, it was the custom that if you came from outside, you would wash yourself and change into something comfortable. You took off your pants and put on a lungi, and just relaxed. Every day you wore fresh clothes.

No one said, "My charge is this much for spending the day with you."

Yesterday, somebody told me, "Did you know that swami charges two hundred dollars per hour?"

I said, "Yes, I'm aware of it. But that's not what I want to do." These kinds of practices only discredit us.

I think each one of us can try to create a place in our home, or wherever we wish, where our friends know they are welcome. In the ashram, for example, people know lunch is served at one o'clock and chai is at four o'clock. They can come fifteen or twenty minutes ahead to be sure they are included in the count.

As society gets more modern and more technologically advanced, this is something we have to think more about. We need more places that aren't bars, where people go to get drunk and stoned and then leave and crash into somebody. We want to be drunk in a different way, stoned in a different way. And that difference is simply love.

So I think you're doing fine. Just keep talking and doing what you're doing.

FILL THEIR HEARTS

Question: We all have people in our lives who try to control how we feel. How do you help those people understand that they shouldn't try to control others?

Gurudev: You can't tell these people not to control others. That is one thing I have learned. As soon as you tell somebody "don't," the person wants to do it more.

I think they do this kind of thing for a couple of reasons. First, they want attention. And second, they want love.

So you have to give these people a lot of love. Fill their hearts. At some point, they will get saturated.

First listen to them, play with them a little bit. You can share stories with them. Slowly, gently, talk with them. It's not that you can simply say, "Okay, now I've told you. Done!" Sometimes it takes a few years, I'm sorry to say.

A little boy comes here with his babysitter. Even though we've become the best of friends, he got angry when he was here the other day. He wanted to latch onto my leg and pull on me. Instead of turning away, I played with him a little. He played with me. Of course, we've done this over the few years that he's been coming here.

I find the same with adults. Adults are big people, but they are just small children inside. For them, control is about feeling they're in power. This is the same whether they are in positions of power or not in positions of power.

On the freeway, everybody knows that cars have to merge into a lane one car at a time. But then somebody thinks, "Why should I wait? I want to go now!"

Sometimes I say, "Okay, let them go." Other times I think, "No. Why should I let them go?"

Sometimes people see how they are acting. It may be too late, but they do see it. Actually, I feel that each one of us always knows what we are doing, even though it may seem as if we don't. A person may say, "Oh, I never knew I was like that!" But I don't think so. I think the person always knew; he just tried to act as if he didn't know.

So, you have to become aware. You see it as a play.

Many people may try to control you. They may try to tell you how you should be, what you should do. Over time, you develop the courage to be yourself.

Over time you also realize such people will always be there. As soon as you fix one, the next one will be ready. It won't end.

For this reason, the most one of us can do is work within our little world, with the people we know. We play with them. We take our time with them. Slowly, we make them better humans. Then, as they go out into their circle of friends, to people they know, they purposely protect what they have received.

When it comes to the rest of the big world, we let God take care of it.

GOD'S WIFE

Question: Baba talks about worshipping the Self. I understand he's not talking about our individual selves, but I don't know how to think of the Self in another, bigger way.

Gurudev: Think of what you did a couple of years ago at the bagel shop. You happened to be there, and you said, "Here, let me pay for those bagels." That's an example of worship, at least in my mind.

In that moment, you had an idea: "This is what I'd like to see happen." And you made it happen. The Self, when you think of it, is present as all the various forms in our lives. That includes the friend whose bagels you offered to pay for.

I read a little story. It's winter, and a rich lady is out walking. She hears a little child talking to God outside a shop. He tells God, "I need a pair of shoes." So she takes him into the shop and buys him some shoes.

At the end of the story, he asks, "Are you God's wife?"

I'm sure she will never forget that moment.

When Baba says to worship the Self, he is referring to the moments all of us have. In each moment, we have an opportunity to worship, to honor, to love, to offer kindness. Of course, we shy away because we think, "What will that person think? What will he feel? Will he take what I give?"

You can't control how someone else is going to feel. But whatever opportunity comes to you, you can go with that.

WINDING DOWN

Question: I'm so busy that I find it very difficult to turn off the thought process and sleep. I don't want to turn off the world, but I need to rest. And I don't know how to do that.

Gurudev: You have to create a timetable for yourself each day: a time to wake up, a time for what you will do in the morning for yourself, a time for the world. And then, when the sun goes down, you decide what winding-down activities you will do until it's time to go to sleep.

It's a matter of preparation—at the beginning of the day, in the middle, and then of course at the end.

People often tell me they can have a cup of tea or coffee and then go to sleep. I don't believe that. I think they are just lying in a supine position, not actually sleeping. I know because when I've done something silly like that, I've lain in bed for three or four or five hours. I may have slept for one hour, but then I woke up and thought, "I didn't really sleep."

You get wise over time. You realize, "Okay, this is the kind of body I have. I'm outgoing and friendly and I like to be engaged in the world." You know that you need to take the last two or three hours of the day to wind down, to do only activities that lead to sleep. The whole evening is geared to that.

I always tell people there is no need for a television screen in the bedroom. There is no need for your telephone. You leave all of that outside. Then when you come into the bedroom, it's a quiet, peaceful place.

You can have some books. You can have music. Especially on a night when you can't sleep, you can read a particularly dense book. That knocks you out; in five minutes you're gone. Other days, you can read a lighter book.

In the ashram, we are in bed by ten o'clock, ready to go to sleep. We know we have to get up at four or five o'clock in the morning, and we want six hours of good sleep so we can be productive throughout the day. Our last tea is at four o'clock, so no caffeine is served during the six hours before sleep. You eat and you chant and then you go to sleep.

The body, I have found over the years, is the best friend we have. As you train it, so it becomes. But you have to train it. You create a schedule for yourself and you stick with it.

Question: I went through a stage where if I ate too much before I went to bed, my heart would beat too fast. I think it might have been too much for the energy. Do you think that could have been the case?

Gurudev: That is probably true for all of us. *Āyurveda* states that we should all eat less as the sun starts to go down. But we don't. We think, "The more I eat, the better sleep I'll get." Then, of course, the body has to work to process that.

I think we should all get wiser and realize that once our noon meal is over, we should start to slow down, because the day is slowing down. That helps the body. It also helps us get up the next morning.

DRAW WISDOM THROUGH YOUR LOVE

Question: I try to listen, but I never quite get some of the lines in the *Guru Gītā*. Is it just a matter of doing it more or is it good to have a lesson on it?

Gurudev: If you can, get a CD of Baba chanting the *Guru Gītā* and listen to him. By listening to him, you'll better understand some of the words.

If you still feel after some years that it's difficult, it's good to get some help. English-speaking people usually find places in the chant where the tongue has to be turned. It's not so easy. If you sit with a teacher who knows Sanskrit, he can help you place your tongue in the right way.

In Sanskrit, the placement of the tongue is what makes the sound. The correct placement of the tongue is also what makes the chant have the effect it should have upon our body.

There are four types of sounds we can make. We have labial, dental, palatal, and guttural. It can take, I would say, a minimum of a month to get the tongue placement so you can make the right sound.

Question: As I remember, Baba changed the melody of the *Guru Gītā* before he took *mahāsamādhi*, but afterwards we went back to the original melody. This isn't a dream of mine, is it?

Gurudev: We are all in a dream.

If you sit with somebody who knows the *Guru Gītā*, that helps.

For example, for the last three evenings, we've been singing the *Pādukā Pañcakam*. Many of you have been singing it for years. Verse number 1 says *pādukābhyaḥ*. However, most people just close their eyes and say *pādukābhyam*. But when you look at the words, you find it says *pādukābhyaḥ*.

Then you read the meaning. The first verse says, "I offer salutations to the Guru's sandals."

Sanskrit is quite a complex language. Anybody who's afraid

of getting Alzheimer's disease, as we discussed at the retreat, can drink beetroot juice—don't spill it on your white shirt—and study Sanskrit. I hope I answered your question.

Question: I'm still not sure about the melody. Has the melody of the *Guru Gītā* gone on for thousands of years or are there different melodies for the same mantras?

Gurudev: The *Vedas* have been chanted the same way. If students study with a knowledgeable teacher for five years minimum, they can learn the correct way to chant the *Vedas*.

But many students don't want to have to live with a teacher for years to learn the things they want to learn.

For example, people come to us and want to learn the harmonium. They want to learn it in one day. They say, "I already know piano. I already know guitar. I already know everything. So just show me. Give me a sheet with the notes, and I'll figure it out." They figure out what they think they should figure out.

In the *Guru Gītā*, for instance, we have *Kailāsa-śikhare ramye bhakti-sandhāna-nāyakam*. Here, *bhakti* has a short i. In English, you don't have different letters to indicate short i's and long i's, and short a's and long a's. You just use the same letter for i and a.

Somebody who plays the harmonium for the first time doesn't understand these kinds of differences. And if that person speaks Austraaalian, it's going to be even more different.

If you are really interested in a language or tradition, you have to go to the country it comes from. Find a good teacher and immerse yourself in the language. Whether it is an Indian language or a European language, that's the only way you will get everything.

As you were sharing with me, there was a man who wanted to learn the didgeridoo. He went to where the Aboriginal people lived, and he was told, "Yes, you can learn it. But for one year you cannot touch it. Just listen to our music. Listen to us. Feel the music first. Then after a year, you can touch the instrument."

People don't always have that much patience and persistence. Sometimes they come to our hatha yoga course and say, "Okay, you're driving me too hard. Give me fewer hours. Let me have the certificate. I just want to go out and teach."

Then they complain that the teacher was horrible. Of course the teacher will seem horrible because the student avoided a lot of the classes and cut practice time just to get that piece of paper. But to get good at anything takes time, commitment, and dedication.

We tend to think that it's only the path of yoga that requires us to have a loving relationship with a teacher, with the Guru. But I think on any path—whether you want to be a carpenter or musician or anything else—you have to have a good relationship with your teacher. You draw the wisdom out of that teacher through your love and passion for learning.

I don't know how it is today when students learn from online courses. But thinking back, when we went through school, I learned the most from those teachers with whom I had a wonderful relationship and who made the effort to be with us students. It worked both ways. We gave a lot, and they gave a lot. Teaching is all about the relationship.

NATURE TAKES CARE OF ITSELF

Question: There's a lot of talk about the shift of the Earth on its axis and that sort of stuff. I was wondering if you might comment on how we can best handle this period, if it's something we need to handle.

Gurudev: First of all, the Indian calendar doesn't end. So according to the Indian calendar, the world doesn't come to an end.

Even for the Mayans—at least this is what the Mexicans tell me—it is just their calendar that ends. In their traditional understanding, the world doesn't come to an end. However, the calendar was made only up to this particular time.

In the Indian tradition, we still have 427,000 years to go. The present age is called *Kali Yuga*. It is only five thousand and some few hundred years old. The total length of the age is 432,000 years. So time-wise, according to the Indian tradition anyway, we have a long way to go.

Doomsday announcements are a good way to make money. People get scared if they think it's going to happen.

I have a little story.

A bird is drowning in a little pond. It is shouting—however a bird shouts—"The deluge is coming! The deluge is coming!"

Everybody wonders, "What deluge?"

Somebody picks the bird out of the water and puts it on land.

By then, word has spread that this bird is proclaiming that the world will end because the water is rising. So somebody goes up to the bird and says, "Where's the deluge? Where's the end of the world?"

The bird says, "Oh, it's finished now."

Because it was in the water drowning, it thought the end of the world had come. But now it is out of the water, it is fine.

Often in our age today, because of the Internet, the media, and the press, people more easily perpetuate these kinds of situations. For example, after you see a movie like *2012*, you have images in your mind that say, "Oh my God, this is what is going to happen." You forget that the writer or director had those mental images and turned them into a movie in which they were played out. Because they were such vivid images, you now carry them in your mind.

Baba Muktānanda would say that we must always be prepared for the end.

None of us knows our moment of death. Therefore, we must always be prepared for the fact that we could die in the next moment.

Often when people hear that so-and-so died, they say, "But we just had lunch yesterday." Or "I just talked to him on the phone this morning." As if having had lunch yesterday or talking on the phone means he could not die. He was normal yesterday. Everything was fine. Yet death occurred.

I think each person faces this uncertainty in life. So rather than pick a date and time when they might die, people think the whole world is going to die at this one time.

One thing we can be sure of: whatever has been created will dissolve. And that dissolution occurs in increments. For example, think of the massive tsunami that happened. It started in one area of the Earth and slowly spread to others. We learned that the animals could feel it coming, so they moved to higher land. Some animals died, but many lived.

We are so inundated with information these days that often we don't know what we really believe. We have to go through a process of sifting and thinking to become clear within ourselves. What is the Truth amidst all the so-called truths?

Actually, the end of the world has been predicted many times in the last twenty, thirty years. But because the Mayan calendar is so well known, many people think the world is really going to end this December.

When the computer was going to go from 1999 to 2000, people thought everything was going to collapse. But then we all woke up on January 1, 2000. I remember going to the computer, and thinking, "Okay, it's supposed to blow up! Or at least it will have the wrong date." But nothing had happened.

Just as we humans make sure things go well, nature also takes care of itself. Consciousness takes care of itself. It does its best to make sure life continues. That's my understanding of what will happen or should happen. We must do good and be good, and then good is what will be there for us.

WHAT TYPE OF DISCIPLE ARE YOU?

Question: Is the role of the Guru important or should we try to find our own path?

Gurudev: We learn everything from somebody. When we want to learn the path of yoga or of spirituality, we must also learn that from somebody. When we learn by ourselves, we don't always know if we have understood it right, if we've taught ourselves right.

Just as there are many doomsday predictors today, there are thousands of gurus. People who have done a little bit of yoga, a little bit of meditation, a little bit of studying with somebody, or who have lived with the Guru for a period of time decide, "You know what? Nobody else in my town is teaching. I will become the local guru." It happens.

So a seeker must be discriminating.

The scriptures teach us about the qualities of a true Guru. When we look for a Guru, we must look for these qualities in the Guru. The poet-saint Kabīr says, "You filter water before you drink it; know a Guru before you accept him or her."

Over the years, people have had bad experiences with gurus. Baba would say that when you buy a case of apples, there will be some bad apples. So the bad apples can tell you what a good apple is. From a bad experience, you know what kind of experience you do want.

At the same time, you don't always throw out the entire bad apple. You cut out the bad part and eat the good part. In the same way, simply because you have had a bad experience with one guru doesn't mean all experiences you might have will be bad. You just say, "Okay, that was that."

In my experience, whatever type of person an individual is, that is the type of Guru he or she will find.

Some people are what you might call traditional or orthodox or disciplined. They follow a method that is traditionally right. Other people decide they want nothing to do with tradition. They think tradition and discipline have no relevance. They say, "I do whatever I feel like doing. I go to bed whenever I feel like it. I wake up whenever I feel like it. I eat whenever I feel like eating. I bathe whenever I feel like bathing." But I think all of us would agree that discipline is good.

For example, if you are driving on the freeway, and the freeway has three lanes marked to go in a certain direction, you go in that direction. Suppose you say, "Why should I follow the lanes? I'll drive in between two lanes." The police will come along and tell you that's the wrong way.

I don't know about here in Australia, but in America, you can't go too slow or too fast. You have to go within the range of the posted speed.

A fellow recently shared with us that last year when he was coming to the ashram, he was going with the traffic. The speed limit was sixty-five miles an hour, and he was going seventy-five miles an hour. Everybody was going seventy-five, so he went seventy-five. A cop pulled him over and said, "Do you know why I pulled you over?"

He said, "I don't know."

The cop said, "Well, you were going fast."

He said, "But everybody was going fast."

The cop said, "You shouldn't go over the limit."

He said, "So why then don't you stop everybody?"

The cop said, "I will stop the others, but for now I've stopped you."

So he got a ticket.

This year when he was coming to the ashram, he was going the speed limit. But when he saw a cop, he slowed down. He was in the fast lane. The cop pulled him over. Again he said, "Do you know why I've pulled you over?"

He said, "I don't know."

The cop said, "You were going slow in the fast lane."

He said, "What do you mean? Last year I got a ticket for going fast and moving along with the traffic."

The cop said, "You should move with the traffic. You're impeding the traffic."

He didn't get a ticket, he just got a warning. He thought,

"Now I'm confused. I follow the traffic, and I get a ticket. I slow down, and I don't get a ticket but I get a warning."

This is why you need a Guru. He teaches you the tricks of living.

Everything is not always the same. You can't make up one doctrine and say, "This is how it is." As I think we all know, in life you have to constantly adapt. You adapt to the country, you adapt to the situation, you adapt to the person.

Often people who read Baba Muktānanda's question and answer dialogues say that two similar questions were asked, but two different answers were given. They think, "Wow, that's amazing!" But we have to realize that two different people asked the question. Those two people were at different places in their practice, at different stages in their life. So the answer was given according to the person who was asking Baba the question.

Sometimes what we ask is different from what we want to ask. When we have a Guru who knows us and with whom we have a relationship, he will answer according to our needs, rather than according to what we think we want.

It's a complex issue, and the Guru-disciple relationship is a complex relationship. Entering into that relationship is not as simple as just saying, "Okay." A husband-wife relationship is not simple, either. Yet if both of them decide they will work something out, it can be worked out.

Often people come to me and say, "He's like that" or "She's like that."

I say, "Look, no matter where you go, he's going to be like that. She's going to be like that. So you already have this problem, you better just solve it." Over time, you learn where you give, where you fight, where you compromise—all of those things.

It's the same in the Guru-disciple relationship. You learn. You become wise. You know what you can do and you know what you are not able to do. You learn all these things, and accordingly you understand that relationship.

Baba Muktānanda wrote a book called *The Perfect Relationship*, which talks about the Guru-disciple relationship. The *Kulārṇava Tantra* talks about it. The Buddhists have many books about understanding the Guru-disciple relationship. The entire *Guru Gītā*, which we sing here in the mornings, is about the Guru-disciple relationship. At first, you understand that relationship at one level, and as time goes on, slowly you begin to understand it at different levels.

In the *Bhagavad Gītā*, Arjuna says to Kṛṣṇa, "You are my friend. You are my teacher. You are my God." We sing verses in the *Guru Gītā* that say, "You are my mother. You are my father. You are my brother. You are my relative. You are my friend. You are everything." I think the whole Guru-disciple relationship can be understood in this way.

When we feel comfortable with the Guru we have chosen, we create that bond, that relationship, that trust.

I think the responsibility lies both ways. Whether it is a yoga school or a church or a temple or an ashram, the people who attend have as much responsibility to make sure the Guru behaves, as the Guru has to make sure the disciples follow the path and the practices. That's why I said, "Whatever type of disciple you are, that is the type of Guru you will find."

Sometimes Indian people tell me, "Well, the times have changed. We can't be as strict as we used to be."

Still, I think Gurus always know that disciples will flunk a little bit. They will cheat a little; they will misbehave a little. Therefore, you set the bar high, so they know they must at least try to reach a certain level.

When you practice different kinds of sports, the instructor says, "Okay, go a little further." The yoga teacher tells you, "Stretch a little bit more." If you are supposed to touch something, you wish the teachers would bring it down so you could grab it. Of course, they know that if they bring it down, you will easily grab it. But if they put it higher, you'll make that little extra effort to get up there.

When the ancient Gurus wrote their instructions for yogic

practices, they knew they needed to tell us to reach a little bit further than we can easily reach.

Question: I've never really understood the concept of ego. I'm confused about why Baba said to try to make the ego go away, and then he said, "If you're going to have an ego, have a big one."

Gurudev: Well, if there's a big balloon of an ego, as you suggest, when it gets burst, there's a big pop. And you are free of it. And if you burst a small balloon, well, it's not as much fun.

Question: I have problems with the idea of the Guru destroying the ego. It took me years of therapy to get to the point of not letting people walk all over me.

Gurudev: Many people like to indulge in what they call "burning the ego."

I'm sure it wasn't Baba's intent to sit there and think, "I'm going to get this one's ego" or "I'm going to crush this one today."

I don't believe that a person needs to be trashed or walked all over. In my experience, Baba never did that to me. And I don't do that to anybody who comes to me, either. That is not what it's all about.

However, Gurus who are into power plays, or who are not truly what a Guru should be, seem to enjoy that sort of thing. That is how they manipulate and control their disciples and the crowds who come to them.

Some people like that. You'd be amazed how much some people like to be walked all over.

I can say this because I'm in this position. For example, sometimes I tell somebody, "Go and do this."

The person has the common sense, intelligence, and understanding to go and do it. But then he comes back and says, "Should I do it this way? Or should I do it that way."

I think, "Just do it." I mean, if that's not the right way, I'll come and tell you, and then we can change it.

In *Cutting Through Spiritual Materialism*, Chögyam Trungpa talks about the steps in this process. First, you go shopping for a Guru, and then you have an affair with the Guru, and third you get angry, and fourth you walk out. And finally you have the realization that the Guru is not just a person or a body; the Guru is in everything in this life.

Any person could say something to you that hurts you or busts your ego. But you won't think too much about it because you don't see that person as your Guru. Nevertheless, the whole process takes place in your mind, and either you learn something from it or you don't. Whereas, when the Guru says something, people make a big deal out of it: "I am going to learn a lesson; therefore, I need to burn."

In the West especially, the whole concept of the Guru-disciple relationship has been misconstrued. When you compare what you hear about the things various gurus do these days with what happened around Baba or Bhagavān Nityānanda or other saints, you realize these current gurus are not in the same state those great beings were in.

FAST YOGA

Question: We're always trying to do things faster in the modern world: we have fast food, so why not fast yoga? So I'm wondering what practices you consider essential, and what are peripheral?

Gurudev: On different days one has different moods. On some days, you want to do something short. You feel that you are already in a good space and practicing for thirty to forty-five minutes is fine. Other days, you feel that you want to practice for two hours.

On Wednesday, we were done after two *sūrya namaskārs*. We didn't want to do a third. The next day, we did five, and we could have done ten. But we told the teacher five because we knew that if we told her five, we would have to do eight.

I think there is a little misunderstanding about fast food. Consider what happens with the packet you pick up in the freezer section of the supermarket. You take it home, and then you thaw it out. Or you put it directly in the microwave. It takes thirty seconds and it's done. But think about everything it went through before it ended up in the freezer section of the supermarket. It didn't just go straight from the farm into the frozen packet. It went through a long process first.

In the same way, whatever end product we might become, our process still has to take place. All of us must go through the process.

The iPhone has an app for yoga. I wish that app would do the yoga and I could just watch and get the full benefit. That would be really instant! Unfortunately it's not like that, as you know.

HONOR THE DIVINITY WITHIN

Question: What do those marks on your forehead mean, and do only men have them?

Gurudev: A woman can wear them if she wants. If you go to the town of Haridwar, you will see women also have them. In some parts of India, women wear white *bhasma*. But mostly men wear them because women are not willing to put so much on their faces.

What I have is sandalwood paste that is freshly ground every morning. Not everybody uses freshly ground paste; many use ready-made powder.

Often I tell people that just as women put on blush and lipstick and all of that as their makeup, this is our makeup.

You can see in Baba's picture that he is also wearing ash. We have fire ceremonies, and the ash that is left over has been purified. When you wear it, it purifies your body because it comes from the ceremonial fire. It protects you because you sing mantras as you put it on yourself. It's like armor.

Sādhus who live on the riverbanks in India have their own little fires, and they take the ash from that. Instead of soap, they use the ash when they bathe. After they come out of the river, they put ash all over their bodies. That's their clothing for the day.

In India, it is the custom to cremate bodies. So every day when you look at the ash, you are reminded, "One day this is what is going to happen to me." One day you will be ash.

Each morning, we bathe our deities. We anoint the deities with sandalwood, bhasma, and different things. Then we also anoint ourselves with whatever is left over after anointing them. The idea is that you honor and worship your deity, and then you honor and worship the deity within you.

We put on three stripes. This reminds us that the world is made of three qualities, or three *guṇas*: *sattva*, *rajas*, and *tamas*. We must learn to rise above all of them.

The red dot, the *bindu*, reminds us that everything comes from one place, one Consciousness. It's said that the morning sun rays are attracted by the redness. The red is made with turmeric and lime. We make it now in our ashram because a lot of the Indian bindis are filled with chemicals.

In the Indian tradition, women wear the red dot especially. Nowadays they wear the stick-on ones and ones with colorful designs. But the idea is that they wear it to honor that Truth, that divinity, within themselves. Mostly in North India—but in South India now too—when a girl gets married, her husband puts red powder in the split in her hair. When you see that, you know the girl is married.

These are all different ways of worshiping. When you look at yourself in the mirror and see what you put on that morning, it immediately reminds you of your divinity, of God. If your mind has ventured somewhere else, you say, "Oh!" Then you come back to the ceremony, to the feeling, to the mantras.

Question: You have taught us to see God in everyone. Does that mean that God is also in Satan and evil? Is violence also God?

Gurudev: I do not believe in the existence of Satan. I do believe that we as individuals, as humans, can create evil. So, yes, in that case, you can see God in that evil.

But when you truly rise above everything, you find there is total equilibrium. There's no hatred. There's no good. There's no bad. These are just qualities we pick up.

We could say it is debatable whether God has created evil or humans have created it. I don't think any scripture says who is the creator of evil. Even in the case of Adam and Eve, who tempted them? Somebody or something did. So God had a hand in it. Somebody has to take the blame, right?

Baba used to tell a great story. One day, the king asked a painter to paint a picture of the most beautiful person; that is, a person who depicts beauty, love, and all of the great qualities.

The painter looked around and found a young boy. He painted this boy's picture and brought it to the king.

The king looked at it and said, "Now paint me a picture of the most evil, the most cruel, the worst person you can find." He described the ugly teeth and all the things we are taught demons have—not that those had to be in the picture, but the person had to have those qualities.

The painter looked everywhere. He went to prisons and to many such places, but he could not find an evil person. Finally one day, he found a young man, and he thought, "Ah, here he is!" So he asked for permission to take this young man to the studio where he was painting.

When they walked in, the young man saw the previous picture. He began to cry.

The painter said, "What happened? Why are you crying?" He said, "I can't paint you anymore. You are not the archetype of evil that I brought you here to paint."

The young man said, "I don't know what to say. Years ago, I was just like the young boy you painted as the best, the most godly, loving, wonderful kid. And today you have brought me as the most evil, the worst person." He said, "I see what I have done to myself. I was the best person and today I am the worst."

Who is it that does this? We do it to ourselves. We make that choice. God makes us and puts us on this Earth. And then through the company we keep, through our friends, through whatever we have in our lives, we take on these different qualities.

Therefore, the scriptures talk about satsaṅg, keeping the company of the Truth. You want company that will uplift you, rather than company that will bring you down.

It is said that a true friend is the one who criticizes you and shows you what you are doing wrong. Of course, you may not like that person, but he is your true friend. And a true enemy is one who praises you even when you are doing something wrong.

God exists in all people, whether they are loving or filled with evil or hatred. The latter have simply covered themselves with the quality of evil. It's like going to the theater and watching a play. They put up different backdrops to set the scene:

a house, the mountains, a forest. In the same way, we put on different facades.

According to the scriptures, everything on Earth is made of the three guṇas, three qualities. Sattva is purity. Rajas is activity. Tamas is inertia, darkness. If you want, you can call tamas evil. They say each person is made of a blend of all three guṇas. There's goodness in us. There's activity in all the things we do. And there's a dark side in us, also. God has created us in this way so we can learn to rise above these qualities and understand that God is greater than all of them.

However, depending on our karma and what we have done, one guṇa predominates over the others. If you live a pure, simple life, sattva dominates because you are clean, you are holy. When your life is filled with activity—as is the case in our society, where everybody is going, going, going, and always wanting more, more, more—rajas dominates. There's never time to sit, to be still, to contemplate the Truth, to contemplate God. There's just drive. And then there is tamas, whereby you don't desire to do anything. You're totally laid back.

In India, I think people need to acquire a little bit of the movement and activity—the aspect of rajas—from the West. And in the West, people need to learn to be a little bit more laid back and relaxed—not to become *tāmasika* but to have more of that aspect of tamas.

You use sattva to rise above all of this. According to the scriptures, as you do sādhanā, you become more and more established in sattva, in purity.

Finally, you come to the stage where you rise above sattva, as well. You become free of all three guṇas. Then, for you, there is no good and no bad. None of these qualities exist for you. What is just is.

When Gandhi was shot, he could have cursed the person. He could have said whatever he wanted. Yet out of his mouth came "*Hē Ram!*" Or "O God!"

Of course, it's not easy to see purity, divinity, in a person who is doing something wrong. It's easier to look at the world and ask, "Why are all these bad things happening? Where is God?"

At the same time, this is the way the world has always been. If you read history, you see that man has always fought, man has always wanted more. It has never been his desire to sit quietly and enjoy whatever is.

Sometimes it's possible to correct a person who is doing wrong by telling him or pointing out a better way. There is nothing wrong in doing so. It's not that you should walk away and say, "Forget it. Big deal. He'll learn his lesson some day." If you happen to be there, you have the opportunity to help.

Here is a simple example. I was by myself, and somebody was coming through the door. So I held it open. As she walked in, she gave me a look that said, "Is something wrong with you? Why do you hold the door open for me?" I didn't say anything. I just smiled. But I could tell from the look on her face that she couldn't believe somebody would be so nice.

These kinds of actions matter because they leave an imprint on people. Whenever somebody does anything nice for you, you remember that. And in turn, you will do it back to somebody else.

For this reason, I always say that whatever you want done to yourself, do it to others first. People will learn from your example.

If you are evil and wicked, that's what you will get in return. If you are loving and sweet, despite all the other emotions that arise, that love and feeling of goodness will prevail. With that, you can wash evil out.

STAY FOCUSED

Question: For a person wishful of attaining the greatest good, what would be the most efficient use of his time around the Guru?

Gurudev: I have to think about that. For one, I would say to stay focused on why you have come to be with the Guru. And build upon that.

When you have a lot of friends, and you're around the people you know, sometimes the mind gets distracted by what others suggest you should do with your time.

You have to look within yourself. Listen to what is taking place in satsaṅg, and then ponder, "What do I want to do so I can get the most good out of my time in satsaṅg?"

Baba would say that the mind has to be clear within itself about why it is here. And I think, through that clarity and focus, we obtain that which we want to obtain.

Question: My addictions are reasonably benign, but chai is one of them. I know we need to get back to the Self, but the objects are so alluring. This is the stage where I'm stuck.

Gurudev: That's why we didn't send you for that cup of chai. Between here and the chai are a lot of obstacles.

I think it's true for everyone that until you arrive at the Self, you encounter all these obstacles.

It's like driving down the freeway. Every few miles there is an exit. If a seeker doesn't become aware, he will take every exit along the way. He'll never make it from Adelaide to Melbourne. That's what happens in life too.

Sometimes I hear, "Oh, so-and-so hasn't been around for a while."

Later you ask that person, "Where have you been?"

"Oh, I got busy with life."

Each and every individual gets drawn to the objects of his pleasure.

In the *Kaṭha Upaniṣad*, Lord Yama tells Nāciketa, "There

are two choices in front of every individual: that which is pleasurable and that which gives the highest good."

What is pleasurable is determined by the individual. As soon as the chai goes on your tongue, you say, "Ahh!" But once you refine your tongue, not all chais are "ahh." Some chais are "pffff." Your tongue has been refined, so it understands the difference between a good cup of chai and a bitter cup of chai, and everything else in between.

I find that most people haven't refined their sense of taste, their sense of smell, their sense of sight, or their sense of hearing. I think, as a seeker, even if you haven't gotten free of the object yet, you can at least refine your senses so you know what objects are best.

For example, this morning's chai was not pleasurable for me, so I just had a little bit. Normally I have a cup and a half, but I had only half a cup. Now the question is, was it the milk? Was it the tea leaves? If you brew it too much, it becomes bitter. There are many factors that a refined tongue considers when determining what is pleasurable.

In today's society, we want shortcuts. Our mothers and grandmothers made chutney on a stone. If you take that chutney made on a stone and you take chutney made in a microwave, they don't compare. But if you've only had microwaved chutney, and you've never had stone-ground chutney, you won't know the difference.

Last night we had a whole tray of desserts.

Someone who was looking them over said, "That one doesn't attract me. And that one doesn't attract me either." So he only took one.

I said, "Why didn't you take that one?"

He said, "Just by looking at it, I knew I didn't want it."

I said, "That's wonderful. At least you have in your own mind decided what is pleasurable."

Otherwise it's like a story Baba used to tell. Mullah Nasruddin arrives in New Delhi from Turkey, and buys a kilo of nice red-looking things. He sits down by a tree to eat them. After he's had a couple of bites, he finds they are quite hot. But he keeps eating.

A local person walks by and sees him with that kilo of stuff and says, "Those are chilies. You put a little bit in vegetables or dal or whatever you are cooking. You don't eat them by themselves."

Nasruddin says, "I realize this is not something to be eaten by itself. But because I have bought it, now I'm eating it."

Baba would laugh and say, "This is what all of us do."

You have acquired an object, and now that object is no longer giving you pleasure. It's only burning your mouth. Your eyes are watering. Your nose is running. You are in terrible pain. But since you have already acquired it, you're going to make sure you get pleasure out of it.

The wise person realizes, "It's not giving me the pleasure I imagined it would."

The discrimination needed is to let go when you realize it's not giving you pleasure. And if your mind is again drawn to that object, remind it of the moment you had that realization. Replay the experience and constantly remind yourself.

In this way, you learn that it is just a game with your own mind. It's not a game with anybody else.

Sometimes when we go shopping and we don't buy anything, I say, "Oh, we've come home rich."

Somebody asks, "Why?"

I say, "Because we didn't spend any money."

I enjoy sense pleasures. The sages don't tell us not to have pleasure. They say have pleasure, but don't be attached to it.

For example, I tell people to feel free to have a cup of chai in the morning. Or have orange juice or whatever they like. Have it if and when you feel like it. It shouldn't be that as soon as you jump out of bed, your mind thinks, "I need chai or I'll get a headache!" Or "Give me a cigarette or I can't go to the toilet!" Or "I need coffee, otherwise…" If it's like that, then you are no longer having the pleasure, it is enjoying you.

Question: I hear that I have to focus. What am I supposed to focus on?

Gurudev: I was told yesterday that there was a game between Mexico and Brazil. The person said, "Guess who won?" The answer was Brazil.

Now, you can ask why one team wins and the other loses. Each player has to do one thing: stay focused on the ball. He can't listen to the applause of the crowds. He can't get lost in anything else. He must think of one thing: the ball. The moment he thinks of something else, even if the ball comes straight to him, he won't see it because his focus is not there.

The first practice we teach is to sit. If one cannot even sit, how can one focus?

When you sit for meditation, you withdraw all your senses. This is *pratyāhāra*. Instead of following all the thoughts that are running outside, you bring your focus within. This takes time to learn.

THE HUNDREDTH SHEEP

Question: We love painting, and we're conscientious about doing our job. But no matter how hard we work, it is harder and harder to get jobs. Will you please tell me what we're doing wrong?

Gurudev: Sometimes it seems as if destiny doesn't favor us. Many people get worked up about this.

Yesterday someone said to me, "I sometimes think I'd like to just sit in one place, study and read, and not go anywhere."

I said, "Yes, the world can be quite selfish."

Each one wants to have the best for himself, but also the cheapest. You can't have both. You can't have the best and the cheapest. When you have the best, it has value. When you have the cheapest, it is what it is.

In our times today, I find good people are not always liked or welcomed. Many people don't know what is good. They just want to go where the masses go.

Often as I travel through airports, I see two sets of escalators. A large group of people goes to one set, and the other set is empty. It gets maybe two or three people. Everybody sees it, but they think the crowd is going to the other escalator so that must be where they should go. It's the same with the immigration officers and at the check-in counter.

I do the opposite. I look to see where it is empty, where nobody is going. Of course, I first read the sign to make sure it's okay to go there.

I would say it's a sheep mentality. One sheep goes that way, two sheep go that way, five sheep go that way—so the hundredth sheep also goes that way. Only a single sheep ventures over to the other side and stands by itself and wonders why nobody is coming along.

My belief is that we must constantly put forth the effort to create our best. At least some people in the crowd will appreciate and value that which is good.

For example, you can make beans in two ways. You can soak dry beans for twenty-four or thirty-six hours and then cook them. I tell our cook to change the water every six hours because the oxygen gets used up. Or you can buy a can of beans, throw them in the microwave, and they're done. Maybe you put out salt and pepper and say, "Add it to your taste." Somebody who doesn't know the difference will think, "Wow." So I think you just continue doing the good work. In its own time, your work will bear fruit.

As you go to sleep every night, tell God, "I'm doing my best." Think to yourself, "I know I've been good." What is most important is that you get a good night's rest, without any worries about something you might have done wrong. I think that is worth a lot.

Question: Do you think that either the Christian or the Islamic religion will ever overcome the level of intolerance they have today toward those who are different?

Gurudev: I don't think the animosity has as much to do with the religion as it has to do with the people.

People who actually practice the teachings they have been given don't have anything to fight about. Nevertheless, people fight in the name of religion. This has always been so.

I was in a small village in India about five years ago. After we finished our satsaṅg, they told me, "If we go now, we will be in time for the evening āratī."

As we arrived, I stopped at a high point that overlooked the temple and courtyard. I saw how many people had gathered for the āratī. Those with fresh clothes were near where the priest was doing the service. Others were standing outside the temple. And some were sitting under the tree in the courtyard. So many people from the village had come just for those few moments. They had all come together in the name of God.

As I stood there, I realized that these kinds of places were created to bring people together.

If you study the teachings of different religions, you will find that all the teachings are basically the same. No religions teach people to fight. They teach us to be at peace with each other.

INNER FREEDOM

Question: For me, freedom has been to express myself, be the person I want to be, go where I want to go, do the things I want to do. I'd like to know what your experience of freedom is.

Gurudev: I think freedom from our whole thought process and from catering to the mind is the first step toward inner freedom. Not being driven by a cup of coffee or by an object, or by a want or a need, is a great freedom.

I often use the example of people who smoke. They can begin by becoming aware, "I am not enjoying smoking; smoking is enjoying me."

Yoga teaches us not to be a slave of the mind. Instead, let the mind be your slave.

Often in life we act as if, as they say, the grass is greener on the other side. We think to ourselves, "If only *that* was in my life." Or if only…whatever it is we imagine we want. Most of life is spent in that pursuit, and we never enjoy that which is right in front of us. The mind is always looking across the fence.

Yoga teaches about inner freedom. You become aware that you must become free from the shackles, walls, and fences you've built within.

You mentioned freedom to express yourself. The *Bhagavad Gītā* says, "Speech has to be truthful, beneficial, and pleasurable."

That means that when each one of us speaks, it has to be the truth. It doesn't mean that you don't care how the other person feels because, after all, you're speaking the truth. Kṛṣṇa says, "No, it has to be beneficial." When the person hears whatever you're saying that is the truth, he shouldn't feel disturbed by it. He should feel, "What I heard will benefit me."

It should also be pleasing to the ear. It should make that person smile, and think, "Oh, yes, that's right."

Often people who follow the so-called path of righteous truth think it doesn't matter what the other person feels or thinks, or how he reacts. They think, "I'm free to express myself, so I'm going to tell him or her the truth." That's not really freedom. They're just passing their pain or their suffering or their torture on to the other person.

Whatever you say—even in the name of freedom—you still have to look at the other person and make sure that it's beneficial, uplifting, and pleasing to that individual.

This applies not just to speech, but to the activities you do.

When you go to any great sage and sit in his presence, have darśan, and listen to his knowledge, you may wonder, "What is it that I experience? What is it that I feel?" If you think about it, you feel uplifted in that presence. In his state of freedom, the sage is aware that each individual must be uplifted, must feel good.

So I think all of us, at the same time as we pursue our experience of freedom, must make sure that those around us are uplifted, as well. Having said that, I'll say it's not easy. But it is possible.

Question: These days, time is speeding up. We're slaves to time. I'm curious how we can become free of the time and schedules and things that bind us.

Gurudev: I think time has always been the same—then and now. We just treat it differently.

For example, before if somebody lived in Mount Barker, the person was just happy to live in that little town. Today, if we meet somebody who is seventy years old and who always lived in Mount Barker, we say, "In his whole life, that person only lived there, and he only knows this." We imply that the person hasn't enjoyed life. But if you ask that individual, he will say he's totally happy having lived in Mount Barker all his life and not having to worry about what's happening in Adelaide.

Some people worry about the entire world—from the time they wake up till the time they go to sleep. And throughout the time they are sleeping. Therefore, they don't find time to help take care of the world. Their *vṛttis*, or thought modifications, are not just about themselves and what is immediately around them but about the entire world. So they feel they have no time. Even if these people want to sit and be quiet in their front yard or in front of their fireplace, they can't. Because the vṛtti in them is "I've got so much to do!"

If this happens to you, throw the question back to yourself: "Who says, 'I have so much to do'?"

You make your own schedule. Your calendar reminds you that you have so much to do. So you can decide with what you want to fill your calendar.

Some people love to fill their time slots up to the last minute. They don't allow themselves even a little bit of freedom within their schedule.

For example, we're going to spend a week in Ganeshpuri at the end of this month, the first week of October. When the trip first began to come together, everybody's question was "What are we going to do for the week?"

I said, "Nothing!"

They replied, "No, we need a plan. If I'm coming, I need to know what I'm going to be doing."

I said, "Well, you go to the temple at four o'clock, which is when it opens. You have the morning prayers, which are till six or six thirty. Maybe we'll do the *Guru Gītā*, so that's seven thirty. Have breakfast. Have a little walk around town. See somebody you know. Check out the different places where Bhagavān lived. Go back to the temple at eleven o'clock to chant and attend the noon āratī. Have lunch. Have a little nap because you've been up since three o'clock. Have some chai. Walk around. Go back to the temple by seven o'clock and attend the evening āratī. Have dinner. Have a little walk. Go to the nine thirty āratī. By then you're ready to sleep at ten o'clock." I said, "That is a full day."

Some people still wanted to know, "Will we do anything else in between? What will happen between the breakfast and the eleven o'clock chant?"

Some people go on a vacation for a week. For the whole

time they're on vacation, they feel they have to keep themselves occupied. Like Nasruddin and his chilies, they want to eat their money. When they come back from their vacation, they need to rest at home because they're tired from their vacation. This is what the human mind does to itself. We have to constantly remind ourselves, "Relax!"

I share a story. A sādhu sits on the verandah of a temple. He sits there for a month.

The manager of the temple sees him there every day. So the manager walks up and says, "What are you doing while you're sitting here?"

The sādhu says, "Sit down. I'll tell you."

Three or four minutes go by. The manager says, "So, tell me." The sādhu says, "Sit. I'll tell you."

After a couple more minutes, the manager says, "Look, if you're not going to tell me, I have to go."

The sādhu says, "I have been sitting here for more than a month. I sit here all day. You can't even sit for five minutes."

I hope you get my point. I mean, what does the sādhu do? He sits.

Baba said, "Do you think that it is a joke to contemplate God or the Truth, or to repeat the mantra all day? Do you think it's easy to sit, to keep your mind focused, to keep your mind aware?"

You may think you want to just sit, but it's not always so easy. As you live life, you may want to put time into your schedule to sit. Of course, then you'll wonder, "What will I do when I sit? Will I have a cup of chai with my friend? Will I think about what I learned in class?"

Contemplation is constantly taking place. But sometimes it happens at a deeper level. So just sitting allows you to wonder and become aware.

When you sit by yourself, you have no music, no television, no phone. You sit for at least thirty to sixty minutes. Remain quiet. Listen to the wind, the rain. Watch the clouds, the sun. See how it feels. Ask yourself, "Am I happy with myself? Do I feel good about myself?"

Wherever you go, consider the effect you have on others as well.

In the *Bhagavad Gītā*, Lord Kṛṣṇa speaks about the qualities of a devotee. He says, "You must not be disturbed by others. Others must not be disturbed by you."

Everyone always tells me, "I can understand 'You must not be disturbed by others,' but 'Others not be disturbed by me?' That is not under my control. How can I control others?"

When you come to understand this verse, you realize both are incumbent upon you. Become a person whose nature, whose quality, and whose temperament are such that nobody is disturbed wherever you go. At the same time, no matter what kind of person comes to you, you are not disturbed because you are established in the Self, in the Truth, in this understanding. That's what you want.

When we go to see a Guru or go to the samādhi shrine of a Guru, we don't go to see the individual, we go to see that which they radiate—the energy, the presence, we experience there.

All this, in my mind, is about freedom, about how we want to live.

VOICE OF THE HEART

Question: What's the best way to connect to the knowledge of the heart, as opposed to the mind?

Gurudev: We are actually so absorbed in the mind that even when the heart speaks to us, we don't connect to that space.

We identify with the mind. The mind is pushy. Its thoughts are constant. The voice of the heart, of the Self, is gentler, softer.

The Self seems to speak randomly. This is because we have so many thoughts that the voice of the Self often doesn't have an opportunity to get through. And when it does, it's in between so many other thoughts that we miss it.

What you have to do is train yourself to listen to the Self, to hear that voice when it speaks to you.

Many people ask, "How do I know the difference between when it is the mind and when it is the heart or the Self?"

There is a clarity that comes when the heart, or the Self, speaks. It happens when you are quiet within and aren't distracted by thoughts. It just happens. With it comes a feeling that nothing else in this world carries. We are aware that the Self within us has spoken.

But sometimes what the Self says is so opposite of what we want to hear that we say, "No, no, it can't be. It's not what it should be. It's not what I want, really." So we don't follow it.

You have to talk to your Self. Understand, "The voice has spoken to me, and therefore let me do what it said." When you can do that, it bears fruit.

It takes time. It takes effort. It takes consistency on your part. It doesn't immediately bear fruit, but it bears fruit in the long run.

The purpose of meditation is to be able to sit and slowly learn to filter out thoughts. You train your mind to have fewer thoughts. If there is less chatter in the mind, then when the Self speaks to you, you are able to hear it.

Question: I have a desire to feel that unity, but it's still very much in my head. I don't know how to transition from the mental knowledge to the inner experience.

Gurudev: One day you just drop into it. Think of when a massage therapist holds your head and says, "Relax, relax."

You think you have relaxed.

The therapist says, "Little bit more." Over time, it clicks and then you just let go. You realize, "Ahh, that's relaxed!"

It is the same with this experience. You understand it now with your mind, but one day the practical application will happen. Until then, you are just aware that that has to happen.

As to why it happens when it does, an astrologer might say it is the right planetary day. Somebody else might say something else. I think that somewhere within yourself, on that day, you simply accept that experience. You accept the teaching and allow yourself to go to the place of oneness, of unity.

Until then, maybe you still have a question. You still have a doubt. You may not even be aware that the question or doubt maintains a little wall of separation. It's like having a sheer curtain. It may not be a thick curtain, but it's still a curtain.

Kabīr says, "Take the veil down and then you'll experience the divine."

We begin with a very thick veil, and then over time as we study, as we understand, as we comprehend, it becomes thinner and thinner.

It's like peeling an onion. We peel off layers. And then one day there is no more layer to peel. On that day the story ends. But sometimes I wonder if we really want the story to end.

Question: Every morning I wake up and I have to find myself again. How do you stay in the presence?

Gurudev: In the ashram, we are surrounded by it. So we have no choice. That is what you have to do too. Surround yourself through music, candles, incense, and flowers, and by keeping your place clean. There are many different ways and means and methods to stay connected all the time.

Question: I do all that stuff and I still lose myself.

Gurudev: You get better and better at it. Some days you have memory lapses. But I would say ninety-five to ninety-eight percent of the time, it is a matter of putting forth the effort.

LOVE YOURSELF

Question: I have a great relationship with my husband, but when I'm on my own I'm very insecure. Can you tell me how I can enjoy once in a while being on my own?

Gurudev: I think it's related to self-love. Your husband has to allow you to love yourself. Each of us has to find a place of comfort in our own company.

You start a little bit at a time. You and your husband can figure out how little that "little" is. For example, maybe he goes to the store and back.

It's wonderful that you have the love you have. You just have to allow that love to become bigger. Know that the same feeling you experience when he's around is there even when he's not physically around.

We could say there is a little switch inside the mind. When you discover how to flick that switch, you have a sense of security within yourself. You know that everything will be fine. You don't need to worry, "What will happen if he's not around?"

Question: I feel I can love everybody else, I just don't know how to love myself. Could you please tell me how to love myself?

Gurudev: Baba would say that the first mistake many people make is they don't love and respect themselves.

Here we say, "With great respect and love, I welcome you." Baba would say, "We have to remember to love and respect ourselves first."

Our prayers say, "May all beings be content." You must remember that when you say "all," it doesn't mean everybody else but you. The "all" includes you. Similarly, when you say, "I love everybody," remember that you also are part of that everybody. Don't exclude yourself.

The question might arise, "Why should I feel love for myself? Why should I feel good about myself?"

Unless you feel good and feel love for yourself, you can't

really give love and share from a place of Truth. Somewhere within you, there's a sense of lack.

You can start by doing an exercise. Take a piece of paper and create two columns: one for all the good things about yourself, and one for what you think are the bad things. Then review your list. You can add and subtract as you go. You may find that you wrote down more good things than you thought you would. You realize, "I do a lot of good things, it's just that I'm not aware of those good things."

One purpose for taking the time to sit alone and quietly is to become aware of the goodness that lies within.

Often when a person who doesn't know much about yoga first comes to satsaṅg, that person starts to cry. He doesn't understand why he is crying, but he may say, "These are not tears of sadness, of pain. I am happy."

If you were to ask, "Why are you happy?" the person might not be able to say. But somewhere within, he was able to go beyond all those layers that have accumulated, and touch the Truth, or goodness, that exists within.

Of course, over the next few days, the layers come back. Sometimes even twenty or thirty years later, people say, "I want the experience I had on the first day."

We could say, there was innocence on that first day. There was a sense of purity. You didn't know what you had connected with. Now you want that again. So you do sādhanā.

The fact that you asked this question means that somewhere within you there is an awareness that you want to love yourself.

Another exercise I give involves a mirror. As you get ready in the morning, talk to the mirror. Smile at your image. Tell it, "You look beautiful. You're wonderful."

We are funny people. We can feel good talking to a mirror. But we hesitate to say the same thing to ourselves. The image in the mirror is not different from you. So remind yourself, "I'm here. And I'm wonderful." Just as you say to others, "I love you," say to yourself, "I love myself." Discover whatever it is that makes you feel that way.

You start by talking to a mirror, and then after a time, that reflection can happen in your life.

SIMPLIFY YOUR LIFE

Question: How can we be seekers and yogis and do all the practices and also lead our mundane lives and professional lives with the utmost fulfillment? How can we reconcile the two?

Gurudev: Baba would say that if you choose to do both, then you must have the attitude that your worldly tasks are also sevā, or service. You see your mundane life as furthering your sādhanā. It's not just "Okay, this is my mundane world in which I have to do things to make money to feed my wife and my kids and my family." You have the attitude that your spiritual experience incorporates and encompasses all of that.

Baba talked about carrying a japa *mālā*, or rosary beads. When the mind gets tense, you put your hand in your pocket and instead of finding a pack of cigarettes, you find the japa beads. You think, "Ah, I can repeat the mantra and my mind will become calm."

Or carry a little picture so you are reminded of the presence of God, the presence of the Guru. Even now, we always keep a picture of Baba or Bhagavān in our cars, or wherever we go. No matter how caught the mind may be in whatever is going on, it is reminded.

Practices are nothing but helpful tools or techniques. If you don't have any tools, it becomes hard. The mind goes off to do things that you later have to undo.

When you are in your own cubicle or your office, all you do is stop, breathe deeply, and reconnect with your Self. Then you are able to let go of any anger, any frustration that has developed. The body may still be shaking, but the mind is somewhat calmer. As you keep doing this, you come to the point where you are able to keep the mind focused, in gear.

In India, we have the four *āśramas*, or stages of life. In the beginning, one is a student, a celibate. Then one gets married. Slowly one moves toward living in a forest, living a simple life. Finally, one becomes a monk. In this last stage, life is totally dedicated to chanting, meditating, and the pursuit of God.

As you do your work in the world, you can move toward this simpler life. As Kabīr reminds us, the things of the world will never come to an end. So you are the one who has to make the decision and say, "Now I'm going to take time and practice, do my sādhanā." For this to happen, you have to start simplifying now. If you wait to start simplifying, it will be much harder. Wherever or whatever situation you find yourself in, learn to adapt.

Question: Many years ago, I learned that the key to yoga is one-pointed focus. These days, with all the gadgets available, people think they can do many things simultaneously, but I understand only two percent of people can actually multitask. I'd like your perspective on multitasking.

Gurudev: I think you already gave the answer. Everybody is doing so much. But if you ask them if they are satisfied, they will say they are not.

If you live in one place all your life, between your home and your job and your garden and all the things you do, I think you are likely to feel satisfied. You know you have everything under control.

Ultimately, all of us have to come back to a place within ourselves and decide, "What is my level of satisfaction?"

The philosophy of yoga would say that you have to gather yourself, not scatter yourself.

For example, when it is time to eat, turn off all the gadgets. Enjoy the taste of the food. Similarly, when you are talking to somebody, turn off everything so you can listen to the conversation.

You see two people—a husband and wife, or two friends—walking together. Both are on their cell phones. That means neither is really enjoying the company of the other.

Ask yourself, "What am I really doing? I made time to be with this person. Am I really enjoying his or her company?"

Somebody was telling me he set the message on his cell

phone to say, "I'm out of range." If he doesn't want to pick up, he's out of range.

We can decide to be out of range. The other person doesn't know whether we're really out of range or not. But everybody's had the experience of being out of range themselves, so they understand.

It is up to us. We have to decide what we really want.

Question: It seems we have an onslaught of technology these days. How does one handle that onslaught from a spiritual point of view?

Gurudev: I think we have little choice because we all use technology. We allow it to be part of our lives.

For example, in India, the cell phone companies need a place for their towers. A poor person who owns a small piece of land and who wants to make money may rent out that piece of land. Then he has to live under that tower. Of course, people talk about the radioactivity that comes from those towers, and even from each cell phone.

As I travel, I often ask people why they don't use a land line whenever possible to make their calls.

They say, "The numbers are in my cell phone. I don't remember them, but all I have to do is click on a name and the phone dials that number."

I say, "It's good for the brain to have to remember the number."

However, technology has made it so people don't need a land line. Many homes I visit around the world don't even have a land line.

But in the case of an emergency, you need a land line. We had this situation at the ashram in Walden after we shifted to a digital phone system. One day the phones weren't working. The repair man said, "Well, when the power is out, you won't have a phone."

I think it is a difficult time. The world is changing so rapidly.

Who can stop it?

Each of us has to make a decision about how we want to live. We can have a simpler life, an easier life. But we have to find a way to do it.

I was walking on the beach the other day. The person with me said, "This is so beautiful. It's just an hour or so from Melbourne. Why wouldn't people want to live here?"

I said, "My experience the world over is that everybody wants to live in or near the city. Why? Whether it's money or access to things or something else, that's the choice they make."

When people come to the ashram in Magod or Walden, often their first question is "How close is your supermarket?"

In Walden, we tell them it's about a twenty-minute walk. In Magod, we say it's about ten or fifteen minutes to get a ride into town.

They ask, "Can you get everything there?"

It is clear what they're used to. It is easy for city people to go where they want and get whatever they want. When you live in the country, you have to plan ahead, make more of an effort. People all over the world have chosen to live a fast-paced life. And corporations are providing them with a faster pace. No single person's decision can change that.

LARKS AND OWLS

Question: I can only pronounce about five words of the *Guru Gītā*. Does it have the same effect if I just listen to it, as opposed to being able to pronounce it?

Gurudev: Definitely. Mantras are sound. Sound, or chanting, can be used to purify the mind.

Whether we are walking or moving things around, we all make noise. Ultimately, we don't want to create useless sounds. What we want to do is produce divine sound. The idea is to refine ourselves through chanting so our mind has only good, useful thoughts.

The *Vedas* say, "O my mind, have noble thoughts." As you listen to the chanting, use it to cleanse and purify your mind, and also your body.

The *Guru Gītā* seems difficult to pronounce, but it is just a matter of learning to move your tongue. I'm sure many of the people sitting here thought the same thing when they first started chanting in the early 1970s or late 1970s or mid 1980s.

Even the simple verse *gurur-brahmā gurur-viṣṇur-gurur-devo maheśvaraḥ* seems like a lot to get the tongue around. You hear it and you go, "Whoa!" But as you keep saying it over time, you find it becomes easier.

Listen to Baba Muktānanda chanting the *Guru Gītā*. We have encouraged people all over the world not to wake up to an alarm or to some noise, but instead to wake up to Baba singing.

I was reading recently that there are larks and there are owls—two kinds of birds. Similarly, there are two kinds of people. Some, like larks, get up and are ready for the day. Others are like owls; they would like the day to start in the evening. If you are one of those who is more like an owl, I think listening to the *Guru Gītā* is a great way to help you wake up inspired.

THE COMPANY OF THE TRUTH

Question: I have been enjoying satsaṅg and chanting for a few years now. I enjoy the peace during and after satsaṅg. How is meditation different from that?

Gurudev: Swami Chinmayānanda says, "Sit alone and enjoy your own company. If you cannot enjoy your own company, why inflict it upon others?"

I love this quote. Meditation teaches you to enjoy your own company. Good company begins with oneself. I am my first companion. My mind is with me at all times. So my mind always has to be good.

Satsaṅg means the company of the Truth. When the sages advise us to go to satsaṅg, that satsaṅg is not just outside, it is also within. All the positive feelings you think come from outside, you must generate within yourself at all times. Then wherever you go, everything will be just wonderful.

We are fortunate that when we travel, we get wonderful people who have decided all they want to do is be peaceful, be joyous, be content. They have decided that everything else they have in life has not given them that which they seek. So they come to yoga. And yoga gives them the teaching "That which you seek is within you, with you, always."

I often clarify, being alone with yourself means no iPod. Sometimes people put on their iPod and then think, "I am alone." No, that is still a distraction. No telephone, no television, no books—nothing. Just you. You close your eyes. You sit and you contemplate, "What is the Self? What is the Truth? What is the divinity that dwells within?"

We meet together in satsaṅg and do all the various practices we do so we can come to a place of quiet and stillness.

That silence is not so obvious in our world today. As we sat here this morning for about twenty-five minutes, a machine of some kind was on. Every time it slowed down, I would think, "Okay, it's going to stop." But then it would pick up again.

I don't know if it happens in Australia, but in India and sometimes in the United States now, the power will go out.

When it goes out, there is total silence, total stillness. Not even the humming of the refrigerator. We forget that even the refrigerator makes a sound.

One of the first things a person realizes when he or she sits is "I have thoughts." For a long time, you didn't even realize you had thoughts. The next thing that comes up is "What do I do with these thoughts?"

In the beginning you have, I would say, maybe a few million thoughts. Slowly, as you sit and become more aware, you think, "I must reduce the number of thoughts." Over time, through the many practices you do, you reduce the number of thoughts until you come to a place of quiet and stillness.

The *Yoga Sūtras* talk about *savikalpa samādhi*, and then *nirvikalpa samādhi*. The sage realizes that for a long time a person is going to have thoughts. In savikalpa samādhi, thoughts are there, but they do not distract or bother you. You say, "Okay, I have thoughts. I can't do away with all of them right now, so at least I can have good thoughts." Slowly you eliminate the not-noble, the not-good, the not-uplifting thoughts. And you make what thoughts you do have into excellent thoughts.

The sage tells us, "May I hear only auspicious sounds. May I see only auspicious sights."

In this world, it's not possible to see only auspicious sights, to hear only auspicious sounds. But you can train your mind so it does not register that which is not useful, that which is not uplifting, which is not auspicious. It just drops these things, lets go of them right then and there.

Nowadays everybody has a digital camera, so everybody takes a picture. They take two or three pictures and then delete what they don't like. Of course, some people keep all of them just in case. But when you become wise, you realize the memory stick only has so much space, so you must delete what you don't want.

We learn the same in life—to instantly eliminate that which we don't want, that which we don't need. All this comes from meditation.

According to the *Kaṭha Upaniṣad*, walking on the path the sage has told us to walk upon is like walking on the edge of a sword. It is difficult to walk on anything as sharp as the edge of a sword. So how do you prepare yourself to walk this path?

The only way is to sit each day. Baba would say to sit for a minimum of fifteen minutes. Or a maximum of an hour, if you can find that much time each day. If you cannot find a single time that is long enough, then at least sit once in the morning and once in the evening for as long as you can.

You set everything aside and begin by taking a look at your day. How have you been? Notice if you are living, as Lord Kṛṣṇa says, in such a way that you are not disturbed by others, and others are not disturbed by you.

As you sit each day for meditation, you eliminate unnecessary thoughts. You ask yourself, "Who am I?" Gradually you become clearer about how you can be a better person so that wherever you go, you can both be enjoyed and enjoy others.

I often ask people, "If you have a choice between going to a play that's joyous and uplifting, and one that is sad, which would you choose?"

Some people become wise and say, "Why would I go to a play that's not uplifting?"

I say, "The natural choice for each of us to make is to be uplifted, to be joyous." That's what naturally comes to us.

The *Upaniṣads* tell us, "We are born out of bliss. We live in bliss. We are sustained in bliss. Ultimately, when we merge, we merge back into bliss."

I'll share a story. Maybe it helps you understand. A couple sit each morning at their dining table and have breakfast.

At the same time each day, a neighbor hangs her laundry.

Each day, the wife at the breakfast table complains to her husband that the neighbor does not wash her laundry very well.

About three weeks into this, when they're having breakfast, the wife says, "Oh, finally she's cleaned her laundry well."

The husband looks at his wife and says, "I cleaned our windows yesterday. It's not that her laundry was dirty for those three weeks; our windows just needed cleaning."

Meditation does the same thing. It cleanses our perception. Baba Muktānanda often said, "The world is fine as it is. It is the prescription of your glasses that needs to be fixed so you see the world as it is."

Ādi Śaṅkarācārya says, "Fill your eyes with wisdom, and then you will see that the world is nothing but Consciousness."

Meditation is something that just happens. It's not something you have to do. Yet as you sit each day, there are three things to keep in mind.

First, learn to sit.

Even after many years of sitting for meditation, many people still haven't attained what Patañjali means when he says, "Your posture has to become still." People say they want to meditate, but they can't even sit. They have to move.

The body has to learn to become steady. It has to be comfortable. Not only physically comfortable, but comfortable within yourself. If you are in a chair, place your feet on the floor. Place your hands on your knees or on your lap. And just sit.

Make this your practice each day. Bring steadiness, bring stillness. Let your body become a good anchor. Get to the point that you are able to sit for fifteen minutes, then thirty minutes.

Second, when you find you are seated, focus on *prāṇāyāma*, the breath.

The *Yoga Sūtras* talk about many different prāṇāyāmas, but you can simply focus on taking your breath all the way down into the abdomen. As you inhale through your nostrils, allow your abdomen and your stomach and then your chest to expand. As you exhale, let the breath go out again from the abdomen, the stomach, the chest, and exhale completely.

While you sit still, use the breath to quiet and still the mind. The breath and the mind are related. When you do prāṇāyāma, you will find you become calmer, quieter.

Third, when you are in this quiet space, use your mantra. As long as you have thoughts, use the mantra. When you have no more thoughts, the mantra will stop. Sit in that stillness.

In that stillness, enjoy your own company. Enjoy the stillness, enjoy the quiet.

If a thought comes, simply witness, simply observe, simply watch. The thought will go away. Then just be in that stillness. All this will come from regular sitting.

People ask, "How long should I meditate?" Some put a timer and say, "I'm going to meditate for thirty minutes." Or "I'm going to meditate for so many minutes."

I don't think you have to do that. Just say to yourself, "I want to sit." As that becomes your natural habit, your body will automatically know what to do. Nature will determine how long you want to sit. You'll find on some days you are able to sit easily and enjoy it. On other days, you can't sit.

People ask, "What should I do then?"

When you feel you can't sit, chant. Do the mantra. But still sit. Don't get up and say, "I can't become still, so I'm going to go and be busy. I'm going to do something else." No.

The body, I have found, is a wonderful tool. It becomes that which we train it to be. And that is up to us.

FORGIVE AND FORGET

Question: Could you talk about forgiveness? When we truly forgive, does it affect us and the consciousness around us?

Gurudev: When you truly forgive, you feel at peace. There is no more agitation. Until that time, you are simply going through the act of forgiving. But when you come to a place of forgiveness, there is peace.

The biggest obstacle to forgiveness is the ego. Each of us has nurtured the ego for many lifetimes. When we forgive, the ego surrenders. We become humble. We accept that what we did was a mistake. We say, "Okay, I accept that."

Forgiveness comes through a process of contemplation. It can take a few weeks or a few months or a few years.

Whether you are attempting to forgive yourself or forgive others, constantly remind yourself. It's difficult because you may think, "I have forgiven," yet the pain is still there. But when you have truly forgiven, the pain will be gone. Nothing in life can disturb you.

In any situation you go through in life, look at whether it disturbs you. Ask, "Why does this disturb me?" And proceed until you get to the root cause of the disturbance. It may not be that particular situation, but something else. Look at whatever it is, and then forgive.

Question: There's a saying, "Forgive, but don't forget." Does that work with remembrance or does it keep us bound?

Gurudev: I think one never really forgets in life. Nature, God, has made us to always remember.

What you want to do is not remember everything at the forefront of your mind. Over time, I'm sure some things can subside.

That is why I said that each time something happens in life, you can look at what the cause is. Ask, "Why is this happening?" Then let it go.

Question: Would you teach letting go to children, as well? There's a lot of politics on the playground.

Gurudev: Many parents today forget that children who are playing sometimes also fight. But then they go back to playing. It is the parents who get caught in "my child, your child; my child, your child."
I say look at them all as children. Take away the "my" and "your."
When we grew up—as was probably the case in societies all around the world—any of our neighbors who was mother-like or father-like could correct us. If we went home and said, "So-and-so auntie yelled at me," my mother would say, "Good." She didn't think there was anything wrong with that.
Sometimes when that auntie's child came to visit, we would want our mother to yell at him. We would try to remind her, "Remember some weeks ago, when she yelled at me?" Tit for tat.
But our mother would say, "Why should I yell at him? He hasn't done anything wrong."
Many parents today forget that they need to think big, not small. Instead of getting caught up in the idea that "my child did wrong" or "your child did this," in that moment, become big. Realize that all the children are playing and having fun with each other.
The children may fight, of course, and run to their parents to get a little bit of love or comfort. But a parent should not get too caught up in that. The child will naturally go back in a few moments and play again.
I think parents have to learn to forgive and forget. Children do it because it is their nature. They play, they fight, they forgive, and then they play again. Adults have to learn from this.
People always think, "How am I going to get back at that person?" But why? If anything needs to happen, nature will take care of it.

PILLARS OF PEACE

Question: When we witness suffering or pain in others, what is the best practice to deal with it?

Gurudev: I think you can only be loving to a person who has suffered or is suffering. You can't subject such people to more suffering or pain. They are already feeling enough suffering and pain. Instead, you have to overwhelm them with love.

As I travel and talk to people about their hard times, they tell me that what they remember most is the good things people did for them at those times.

Many years ago, a woman who was preparing to give a talk in the ashram had a dream of Baba. In it, he came to her and said, "Say these things."

She said, "But my talk is ready."

He said, "No. People already know about suffering. They already know about pain. They want to know about good things, positive things. They want to know about love."

These days, everybody talks about terrorism and all the crazy things happening in our society. I say, "Those of us who love peace—or at least who say we love peace—are lazy."

People laugh and say, "Lazy?"

I say, "The people who cause terror are working constantly to cause terror. We have to ask ourselves, 'What am I doing to bring about peace? How much effort am I putting forth for peace?'"

We read the newspaper and we say, "Oh my God, the world is becoming terrible." But we are part of this same world.

It is up to us to carry *dharma* into the world. Each one of us—ourselves, our children, our family, our friends—can become pillars of peace, pillars of love, pillars of joy.

I often ask myself why we see so much pain and suffering in the world these days.

My answer is lack of love. I've come to the conclusion over the last thirty years of doing this work that no matter who we are, no matter what part of the world we live in, each of us wants love.

I give the example of a dog. Anyone who has owned a dog knows that you can yell at the dog, you can get angry at the dog, or you can just call him. Whatever you do, he immediately comes to you. He licks you and wants to be all over you. He forgets that you've just yelled or been angry at him. All he wants is that you love him.

It is the same for humans. Often people who came to meet Baba Muktānanda had no idea about his spirituality, his yoga, or his meditation. The one thing they still remember years later is that they got love from him.

Before he took samādhi in 1982, Baba had an orange vest. Of course, he was a few sizes smaller than I am. I had the name of the tailor in Los Angeles who made that vest. So when we were there two and a half years later, I took it to him and said, "I want one like this."

He looked at it. "Ah," he said. "Indian man. Sweet ball."

I realized Baba must have given him a *laddu*, a sweet ball. He was a Chinese tailor in the middle of Los Angeles, and he had come and measured Baba and stitched the vest for him. Two and a half years later, he still remembered the laddu. What he really remembered was the feeling he experienced. But we as humans sometimes are afraid to express love. So we just remember the sweet ball.

I think each one of us has a special quality. We have to figure out a way to give it to others. Wherever we go in society—whether it's with family or friends or anywhere else—we have to bring that quality we have and offer it.

In America, they have what they call a potluck. Everybody brings something he or she made at home: a salad, a cookie, a noodle dish, rice. People love it because you get a variety of foods. You can have a little bit of each kind.

You can see the quality of each one's love. Some people are generous and bring a lot to the potluck. Others are stingy and bring a little. They say, "Oh my God, they've brought so much. I've brought so little. Will there be enough?" That's a fear some people have. I always tell them it doesn't matter. It will sort itself out.

Each of us has to learn to be loving, to be kind, to be forgiving, to be all the positive qualities we want to see in society. Pain and suffering are there. What we want is love.

Think to yourself, "What is it that I can do?" Whatever your quality or your specialty is, bring that with you and share it. And people will enjoy it.

BABA GAVE US A LIFESTYLE

Question: I need to work twice as hard as I have been to make a living and also do sādhanā and meditate. What do I do to establish the discipline to get it through my hard head?

Gurudev: You could take your hard head off.

I think we all have different natures; that's what keeps life exciting. Over time, we become aware of our shortcomings and also of certain things that are the way they are. And we consider, "Okay, what things can I change?"

Mostly, I think everything can be changed. But there are some things that we are willing to make the effort to change. And when it comes to other things, we are stubborn. Sometimes we're not aware of the stubbornness within us that doesn't want to change.

Living together in society, especially when we have skirmishes with each other, forces us to decide what we want to do. Do I really want to change? Do I want to become better at living with others or do I want to stay the way I am?

As we drove up the coast, we stopped at San Simeon, where we saw the elephant seals. For ten months of the year, they are out at sea, hardly touching land. Then for two months they come onto land. You can see them lying on the beach close together and on top of each other. Some weigh more than four thousand pounds. You wonder, "Could humans actually get along with each other in such a close space for two months?"

Yesterday we were discussing the situation in society today and the many things that are going on. The question that arises in many minds is why? What triggers a person—as we saw two weeks ago—to go into a movie theater and kill people? A few days ago, they found somebody else with a gun and ammunition. What he was going to do is not known. But what is it that triggers people?

We all seek love. I think what has happened in modern-day society is we have cut love off. We give love in measured ways now. We say, "You can visit me from this time to this time. And I'll be kind and loving to you at that time." Then we look at our watch and say, "I think my time to give love is up. Your time to be here receiving my love is up. Bye!" But what if either the person giving love or the person taking love is not done? So we develop these hard heads. You're not the only one. We have all developed different means along the way to protect ourselves from society and safeguard ourselves so we don't get hurt. Often I hear people say, "I don't want to get hurt." That's why I used the seals as an example. They snap at each other. We saw that. They play with each other and they also fight with each other. Yet there's a sense of trust.

Baba gave us the discipline. What I think he actually gave us was a lifestyle. If you are able to incorporate that lifestyle into your daily routine, there is nothing more wonderful than that. See if you can figure out in your hard-headed way what things you can do that work for you. Then slowly you make it better.

The *Upaniṣads* say, "Don't be lazy."

Since ancient times, humans have been lazy. So the Guru always advised his disciples not to be lazy. That tendency continues even more in our times today. We have to find ways not to be lazy, to be productive for ourselves and for others.

Question: I want to ask you to please give me a spiritual name and bless me so every time I get lost, I repeat it and can come back to this time, this love, and your presence.

Gurudev: You've put me on the spot!

This matter of spiritual names is a saga we were discussing some days ago. In truth, there is no such a thing as a spiritual name.

In India, the parents and the priests find out the letter for a child's name based upon the time of birth of that child. In some places, they give three names. A fourth one is also given, but it is kept private and only used for pūjās and ceremonies. One name is usually used within the family, and another is used outside in society.

My theory is that when people first came to Baba in the 1970s from the West, it was difficult for a sixty-two-year-old man who didn't speak English to pronounce their Western names. They had names like Margaret, Elizabeth, Russell, Terry. It was easier for him to say, "Your name is Gopi. Your name is Damayanti. Your name is Gopal. Your name is Ram."

People thought, "Wonderful! My Guru has given me this name. I have a new identity." But it was practical.

Of course, as more Westerners came, they had identity crises. They thought, "If he is Ram and he is Gopal and she is Damayanti and she is Leela, then who am I?"

In the beginning there were twenty-five, fifty, seventy-five people. But by the time of the third world tour in 1978, we had a thousand people every night. And out of the thousand, some percentage—I don't know how many—asked for names.

So Baba gave them a name.

But then they said, "What does this name mean? How do I apply this meaning in my life?"

So Baba had two business card holders next to him with name cards. When people asked for a name in darśan, whoever was working with him would pull a card. The card had the name in Sanskrit and in English, and the meaning on the back.

A few years ago, we did something simpler. We had a form and we told people, "So that we can respond to your request for a spiritual name, please send an email and write in the subject line 'request for a spiritual name.' Please send your picture with the email." Of course, some people didn't like this.

One woman said to me, "I need a name."

This was outside, after we had finished the program. I said, "Well, there's a form you can use."

She said, "Then I don't want one."

We have tried to come up with a wise solution. For a while, we only gave names for newborn babies.

As long as people are involved with the spiritual path, they associate with the name they have been given. But on the day they turn away from the path, their blame always goes to the

Guru. They say, "He took away so much of my life. He took away my name and gave me another one. He gave me a different identity."

The Guru had nothing to do with it. He just got caught in the māyā. To simplify his own life, Baba created cards. We created an email. Yet we get in trouble. Truly speaking, you come onto this path to become nameless. Vedānta says the two things that bind us are form and name. When do you get a name? When you have a form. And that form is what you get when you are born: the body. So your parents and relatives want to call that form something.

In India, sometimes it takes three or four years to get a name. In the meantime, while they're waiting for the priests and elders of the family to come up with a name, the baby is called Nino or Nina or Nini, or something like that.

Personally, I think that at some point, the spiritual name business should be abolished. Because the truth is, some people make it a power game. Of course, that is a small percentage of people. Most people are straightforward; they just want to practice and have a spiritual experience.

If you go to the village where Bhagavān Nityānanda spent the last thirty or so years of his life, you will find three or four main places where he lived. The book about his life tells us that every time somebody in one place gained control, he moved on.

His manner was very simple. He either lay on a piece of stone or sat in one of those chairs with the handles that come out and you can put your legs on top. Or he walked. Those were the ways he would be if you went to meet him.

There are teachings that supposedly were given by him. I assume he gave them during the earlier years of his life. By the time he came to Ganeshpuri, he had become quiet. He probably realized there was no point in saying anything.

People only listen to what they want to hear. Even if a teaching is written, they only read it in the way they want to read it. For them, it has nothing to do with the Truth. It has nothing to do with God. It has nothing to do with seeking the

Truth. Everybody's view is colored. We view everything in life through the color of the glasses we wear.

It is said Bhagavān Nityānanda gave one talk for forty-five minutes on the day of Guru Pūrṇimā, about twelve days before he took mahāsamādhi. You can find it on YouTube. Since I never heard him speak, I cannot guarantee that it's really his voice.

In the early days, a Guru sat with a few disciples. The Guru stated the teaching, and the disciples repeated it. The Guru said the teaching again, and the disciples repeated it four or five times. That is also how priests learned their mantras. Nowadays they have books, but in the earlier days they had no books. They had to listen and remember.

Some of our scriptures are called *śruti*. Śruti means that which is heard. The *Vedas* are śruti because they were revealed to the sages. Another type of scripture is called *smṛti*. Smṛti means that which is remembered.

Baba's *Play of Consciousness* we would have to call a smṛti scripture. During his nine years of sādhanā, Baba had many experiences. In a space of twenty-one days, he dictated his account of his experiences, and his translator then wrote the book. Baba was passionate about writing that book. He couldn't get up early enough to work on it. I think the translator probably got tired because there was no computer. It was all done with a fountain pen and paper.

I spent five days in Baba's company during that period. It was our school vacation, in the month of May. Everybody in the house had to be quiet because any noise was a distraction. In the afternoon, the translator would read what had been written that day to the few of us who were there.

In 1979, we were at the ashram in Oakland. One of the sevās I had was to translate for Baba's secretary. The secretary brought Baba's letters at three o'clock each afternoon. Baba would get up from his nap at two thirty. His whole day was like clockwork. The time he got up, the time he had breakfast, the time he showered, the time he did his pūjā—everything was set.

If you were one of Baba's attendants, you had to be ready

ahead of time with the delivery of whatever Baba needed. For instance, his juice was at 10 a.m. At 9:59, you had to be next to him with his juice. Because at 10:01 it was late. Such was his discipline, and that is what he imparted to us.

One day at three o'clock, I went to his room for the translation sevā. Baba was busy reading. I walked into the room. I stood for what I think was minutes—but it was probably barely seconds—and waited for him to look up. I, of course, was very scared of him till the end of his life.

He never looked up.

I went back out. I told his attendant, "He's not looking up."

He said, "Make a noise on the carpet."

I went back and ruffled the carpet.

He still didn't look up.

I went back out to the attendant. He said, "Walk to the bathroom and back, and make noise all the way."

So I did that.

As I was walking out, Baba looked up. He said, "Hmm." Then he went back to his book.

I told the attendant, "I'm going. If he wants me to come back, I will be downstairs. You can call me."

I was only sixteen or so at the time, and I thought, "Wow! You can be so immersed in what you are doing that no matter what is happening on the outside, you can't get distracted." I learned the power of focus.

We get so easily distracted.

People have a little bit of knowledge, and they think, "I know so much." They do a little bit of practice, and they say, "I have done so much." But when you look at their life, you find they have barely done anything. Having lived with Baba, at least, it seems like so little. It is just the ego that thinks, "I have done so much."

Sometimes people say, "There is so much śakti!"

Those of us who lived with Baba know what a lot of śakti is. I don't say this from a place of ego, but from a place of great fortune.

In the United States, when you go to an ice cream shop, you ask, "Can I have a taste?" The person takes a very small spoon and scoops a very little bit of ice cream and gives it to you. Some people eat a few of those spoonfuls and feel happy. They don't want the full scoop of ice cream anymore because they feel they've had their ice cream. But they don't get the experience of saturation.

Sometimes people who have had just a little taste, or a glimpse, of śakti say, "Wow, the śakti!"

I think, "If only they could really know what śakti is." I pray that they will learn to keep moving, to go further, so they can become saturated with the experience.

These days, many people have had a little glimpse. Thanks to the Internet, overnight these disciples become gurus. It's as if they never tasted ice cream—or śakti—and they were given a little spoonful, and went, "Wow!" Then they write a blog. And some other naïve individual reads that blog and adds to it. And before you know it…

A story comes to mind. It's called "The Nose Cutters' Club."

Tonalli is ruled by a king. A woman arrives in Tonalli and announces, "I have the ability to give you the experience of God. Just like that, you will have a glimpse!"

There is one condition given: the person must never have sinned or performed a wrong action. If he has sinned, he won't have a glimpse. Moreover, if somebody doesn't have an experience of God, that person's nose will be cut.

Of course, everybody is very excited. The king, especially, is tempted. But he thinks, "I know I've done some not-so-perfect things."

So he sends his prime minister to the woman.

The prime minister is taken inside the room. The curtain is closed. Shortly, he comes out dancing. "I had a glimpse! I had a glimpse! I had a glimpse!"

The king is not sure his minister is speaking the truth. So he sends his next minister. In fact, he sends his twelve closest ministers.

Each one comes back saying, "Yes! Yes!"

The king still doesn't trust, so he sends his wife, the queen. He says, "I know she will tell me the truth."

She also comes out saying, "Wow! What a glimpse! What a glimpse!"

The king thinks, "Okay, the ministers, my queen—everybody is having a glimpse. I can also have it." So he goes. He comes out. He also says, "Wow! Wow! Wow!"

That night, the queen and he are by themselves, lying in bed. He says to her, "Now, you tell me the truth. What actually happened in that room?"

She says, "You are the king. You tell me first."

He says, "Well, nothing happened. I didn't see anything."

She says, "The same is true for me. But why did you say what you said?"

The king says, "You and the ministers and everybody else said they had a glimpse. So I thought, 'Why should I be the only one left out?'"

The next morning the king can't wait to ask his twelve ministers their stories. Of course, he tells his story first.

Then they all say, "O King, this is exactly what happened to us."

He asks, "But why? Why did you do this?"

They say, "We didn't want our noses cut. And we didn't want the world to think we have sinned or done something wrong. Just as you wanted to protect yourself, we wanted to protect ourselves."

So the king arrests that woman and tells her never to do such a thing again.

This is how the world goes today. Of course, it's not just today that this is happening. Baba and his predecessors told this story, so this sort of thing must always have happened. However, the modern media has made it possible for such people to come up faster.

Baba used to quote Kabīr, who said, "Just as you filter your water before drinking it, test a Guru before you accept him."

The *Kulārṇava Tantra* tells us the qualities a Guru has, and at the same time, the qualities a disciple has.

A master gives us a way to live life, a way through which we can integrate the teachings and make them part of us. Baba's specialty was to offer a direct experience. That is what people received in his presence. It was not just a miracle or magic. He showed us how to practice and live the teachings he gave.

Over the years, I've come to believe that any true master who gave his disciples that experience during his lifetime continues today, even years after his physical form has gone, to share that experience.

You have to take that experience with you as a deeply ingrained part of yourself. You don't actually need anything to remind you of that experience. You are simply able to go to that place inside, and feel that the experience is alive.

As I travel, people often say, "Tell us the best thing about living with Baba." Or the best story. Or the best experience.

I always say there is no one thing I can say was the best. If I say one thing was the best, then what about the rest? I feel fortunate to have had the twenty years I spent with Baba.

I think having the company of the Guru for a period of time is not just a matter of good karma. I have noticed that some people who met Baba are still seeking, still looking for something. When I look inside myself, I find contentment. Through Baba's grace, that contentment has become part of my life.

So create a lifestyle that makes it possible for grace to always be part of your life.

BE DOUBLY GOOD

Question: When I try to stop myself, my mind can get caught in a knot: "Oh, I'm not supposed to think that." This whole thing starts going inside my head. Do you have any thoughts on that?

Gurudev: First become aware of the kinds of thoughts you have. Then slowly, over time, you can learn to change the quality of those thoughts. Gradually, you come to a point where the mind only has good thoughts.

So, first the quantity of the thoughts, then the quality of the thoughts.

I sometimes wonder, "Is it possible for one to always, always be good?"

I see such people around the world. They are not necessarily great sages or saints; they are normal people who live in the world. Through whatever practice they have done, they have trained themselves to always be good. Even when they see somebody else not being good, they find a way to make that person seem good.

The Universal Prayer says, "May the wicked become good. May the good become noble. May the noble go toward peace. May the peaceful become free." The sages believe it is possible.

The people who come to satsaṅg are not wicked. They are already at least good people, noble people. Now they want to become peaceful people. They want to be constantly peaceful.

All the thoughts they have—everything they read, all their conversations, all their dealings—must be peaceful. That takes effort.

If somebody agitates you, you have to remind yourself to remain peaceful. The tendency to correct that person or to say something to him is there. You have to tell yourself, "That's not necessary." This is *viveka*, discrimination.

Discrimination has to kick in instantly, before your reaction happens. The quality of discrimination has to be there in the same way that insurance kicks in when you have an accident.

Slowly, this becomes a natural process within yourself. You don't have to think to yourself, "I don't want to be bad. I want to be good." That fight is over because now you are at peace.

I'm sure if you look back over the year and think of where you have traveled, you will find that you are a better person now. Not that your were bad before, but you got better along the way.

In all the various situations that arise in life, it is so easy to do whatever tempts us. In that moment, you have to remember, "No, I'm going to do good. I'm going to be wise. I'm going to be uplifting."

For this, each of us—as humans, as teachers, as parents, as friends—needs encouragement. We need love from each other. We need positive feedback. When somebody tells you what is good and reinforces whatever you do that is good, you more readily continue to do good things.

I would add that it is helpful to encourage others by saying, "Come this way. Move this way. Come here." Don't say, "*Don't go there.*" As soon as you say, "Don't go there," the person thinks, "Where is it that I shouldn't go?"

When a person is on the street and a car is coming, we don't tell him get out of the way of the car. We say, "Step here." And the person automatically moves over. It is only when the car goes by that the person realizes, "Oh my God, thank you! You saved me."

Question: At school, at the office, in corporations, we meet people who are telling lies. Do we try to change them, to fight the injustice? Or do we ignore them, stay quiet, and try to see the good in them?

Gurudev: I think many businesses teach people to lie.

I was watching a YouTube clip of a swami who was talking about an ad. In it, a woman is taking a shower, singing away. Her husband comes with a bar of Zest soap and gives it to her. He's singing too. He is singing outside, and she is singing in the shower. Then the woman comes out. Her child is there, ready and waiting.

The swami asks, "What does the bar of soap have to do with the wife being happy? Or the husband singing? Or the child being ready?"

There is no relationship in all this—other than that the wife is happy, the husband is happy, and the wife hopes that every time she uses Zest soap, the child will get ready. When I saw the video, I thought of exactly what you're asking about. This is how corporations play with our minds. And we are gullible because we buy what they are trying to sell us.

Somebody was telling me that when her child eats his cereal, he has to have the box with him. There is a game on the box. If the game is not there, the child will not eat the cereal.

We as consumers fall for these traps.

Sometimes when parents come to the ashram for a retreat, they bring a box of cereal and say, "This is what my child will eat for breakfast."

The ashram managers get confused. They have created a menu, so they tell the parents they want the child to eat what the ashram is serving.

The parents say, "No, my child needs this." They continue the lie the corporation has created by saying, "This is what my child will eat."

When you think about fighting injustice, I don't think it's as easy as saying, "I know he's lying. I will fix him." Because he also knows he is lying. As I said earlier, we as humans have to think and ask many questions of ourselves.

Somebody was telling me he's trying for a promotion. He said, "It's just a matter of time before one of my older coworkers retires. I'm next in line to be promoted." But then he said, "That coworker hasn't been coming to work and she won't retire. I don't want to quit because I don't know where else I would go." He said, "Please pray for me."

I laughed. I asked, "Should I pray that she retires?"

Ultimately, you can't look up and down to see how others are. You can only look at yourself. You can ask, "How can I be different?" By becoming better yourself, you can invoke those qualities in the people around you. If you think, "I want him to be good," you have to be doubly good for him to become good.

The conclusion I've come to is that it never works to tell somebody, "I want you to be good." That just makes the person defensive. Then no matter what you say, he won't listen.

So be good yourself. Be humble yourself. Do the right thing. If you see something wrong, try to shift or change or correct it. If you can't do that, simply walk away from that situation.

A similar question that comes up is why, in the *Bhagavad Gītā*, Kṛṣṇa told Arjuna to fight. Each person has a place in society. Each one has a job that needs to be done. Arjuna was a warrior. If you think about the warriors in our society today, you might think of a policeman. The job of a policeman is to stop a person from doing wrong, take him to court, and put him in prison. In ancient times, the job of a *kṣatriya*, a member of the warrior caste, was to correct injustices so that right action could prevail.

You might think there is no longer a caste or class system. It still exists. Only the names have changed. There are still people who are caretakers of wisdom. There are people who take care of the laws. There are people who do business. And there are people who drive the garbage trucks, who clean up after others, and who do menial things. Society always has people who perform these different kinds of necessary jobs.

You can't say, "He can't do that job" or "She shouldn't do it." According to our destiny or upbringing or mindset, each of us performs whatever job we do.

The sages teach us, "Whatever your job is, do it in the best possible way." So, whatever you are doing, do it to the best of your ability.

Question: In the process of doing good, will there be a shift? Will it become automatic at some point?

Gurudev: Correct. For example, when we grew up around Baba, everything was always clean. He believed that if the external circumstances were clean, then what was within would automatically become clean. So he told us to make sure everything was clean: what we wore, how we looked, what was around us.

We still do that in the ashram today. We clean on Friday before everybody comes. We clean on Monday after everybody goes. And we clean in between to maintain the purity and cleanliness.

Two years ago, a woman visited when we were cleaning the basement. She said, "You guys are like my mother."

We said, "Why?"

She said, "My mother makes us clean before the cleaning lady comes." And she said, "My mother says the cleaning lady never cleans the way we want it done. So we clean and prepare and make it nice, and then the cleaning lady just has to tidy up."

Unless you have experienced this kind of cleanliness, you will never understand what clean really is.

In some of the temples in South India, one practice—or penance—that visiting devotees do is to not to use a leaf plate. Their food is served directly on the marble floor. They want to feel oneness with God. If everything is God, why should they need a leaf plate?

We never did that in the ashram with Baba. However, he would say, "My kitchen floor is so clean that you could eat off it."

One of the first sevās that people who came to Baba in the 1960s and 1970s were given was to clean the toilets. They would get a toothbrush and clean away. One fellow shared that he had cleaned a toilet and then stood back and was enjoying how well he had done his job. Just then, somebody walked in and used it. He said, "Okay, that means now I have to clean it again."

Doing sādhanā teaches you to see where there is filth. Then you clean that filth. It gets clean, and then it gets dirty again. Clean and dirty, clean and dirty. You get to the point where it doesn't get dirty anymore.

You find at some point that you are no longer driven by the mind. You become the lord of your own mind. Kashmir Shaivism talks about this. What is the mind, actually? The mind is nothing but Consciousness. Right now it does not appear to be Consciousness because it is caught in māyā. Therefore, you want to purify it so you know it is Consciousness and you can experience it in that way.

THROUGH LOVE, DISCIPLINE

Question: As a parent, am I supposed to take on the role and mold my kids? Or are they going to be molded anyhow with God's grace, and I'm just supposed to hang back?

Gurudev: Any good parents here? I tell people we now have seventy-six boys at the ashram in Magod. And it's a constant challenge. We have eight male teachers, a couple of female teachers, and some ashram managers. I've watched all of them and how they play their roles.

I am a bit removed, yet I allow myself to play a role too. I have found that love is the best means. This is what Baba did, also.

Through love, you discipline. Don't think love means you don't have to discipline. You can still be stern. You can still be clear.

Of course, a child will always try to test you.

You say, "Sit here for five minutes."

At three minutes, he will start: "Is five minutes up?"

You have to be clear: "No." He knows the five minutes are not up. If at four minutes you say, "Okay, five minutes are up," you've lost the battle. He has won, and he knows that next time he can win again.

The discrimination, viveka, is to know not to get angry.

In Magod, I often say, "If one doesn't do mischief as a child, when is one going to do mischief?" If an adult is doing mischief at fifty-seven years of age, then his parents didn't allow him to do mischief when he was little. We have to remind ourselves, "I was there one day myself. I did similar things." Each one has to go through the process of learning, of growing up.

Of course, there are good kids, okay kids, bad kids. You want to try to mold all of them into good kids. I would not say don't try to mold them.

For example, we have one student who's been with us for ten years. When he came to us, he had failed the tenth standard. In India, when you fail, you have to wait a year before you can try again. Originally, he was only going to stay in the ashram for a few months. But he began to work hard with us in the eighth standard. And since then he's come all the way up. He's one of the students who has put forth great effort. He speaks excellent English. But I'm sure, as I often tease him, there were many times he wanted to run away. I tell every child, "Don't try to run away. Tell us what the problem is. Let's discuss it. Let's resolve it."

Recently it occurred to me that since this student has done so well, we should find a way to further inspire him, and use him to inspire those who are coming up behind him. The idea is to bring him to the United States and put him through a masters and PhD program. Of course, that won't be easy. We are still looking for a university that will support it.

When I look at my own life, I think "When I was growing up, I could have gone many different ways in life." But thanks to Baba, my parents, and some of the elders—and thanks also to the fear we had of our elders—I was molded in the right way.

People lack that fear in society today. Whether they are adults or children, they have no fear of their elders. They think, "I can do whatever I want." Therefore we see some of the crazy things we see happening today.

A child's fear doesn't have to always be negative. Fear can also arise out of love, out of respect. It depends upon the adult.

The challenge for each parent—and for each of us as we deal with anybody, whether child or adult—is to avoid being too rigid in our demands. This is where discrimination comes in. You are gentle. You are clear. You are firm. Then again, you are gentle.

A child always tries not to have to do what you want. I have a child who doesn't want to study. I've made it clear to him that he will study up to the twelfth standard. I said, "When you're my age, you will appreciate it. If somebody asks you, 'How much did you study?' you can say, 'I studied up to the twelfth standard.'"

He said, "But I don't like to study."

I said, "I understand. I can relate to that. But we have to look at the long term."

Every few months, I asked him, "Are you studying up to the twelfth?"

Now he tells everybody, "I'm studying up to the twelfth." That has become his mantra. But he told me, "Once I've finish the twelfth standard, I'm going to drum, I'm going to cook. No more Sanskrit. No more studying."

I said, "That's fine."

My goal is that the security guard of the ashram, the driver of the ashram, everybody at the ashram speaks Sanskrit. We will have an educated group of people. Of course, it won't happen overnight.

When you deal with your child, you have to constantly remind him that you are looking at the big picture, at the long-term result.

The other day, I asked a child who is eleven years old, "What are you going to do when you grow up?"

He just shrugged.

Somebody might say, "He's too young to know." But I think eleven is not too young to have ideas. It's not too soon for adults to spend time with him and encourage his ideas. By the time I was eleven or twelve, I knew what I wanted to do in life. I'm not doing it now. But that doesn't matter.

Even as adults, we need molding. Sometimes people want to take a gun and go into a movie theater. Of course, that's the extreme. Still, they should have the right coach, counsel, or friend, whom they can call and say, "I feel that I want to go do this." They need somebody they can talk to who will talk them out of whatever they want to do, who can share with them why they shouldn't do it.

Baba often talked about keeping good company. Through the company they keep, people mold each other.

As we were driving here, we passed a Universalist Church. A couple of Buddhist monks were coming out of the program there. It's wonderful to know that every few blocks, people are joining together for satsang and meditation. They are learning about what they should do and what they should not do.

I think more of this needs to happen. All of us have to find ways to develop our good qualities. It's a challenge for each and every one of us. Parents can make sure that at least on the weekend, or one day a week, their child goes to satsang or to someplace where he is exposed to wisdom, to culture, to language.

First, you need clarity in your own thoughts. "What exactly is it that I want?" A child picks up immediately when you're not being clear. Second, you need to be able to express that. If you realize as you are expressing something that you are not clear, say, "Wait a minute. I need to become clear on this."

For example, in India, when you ask, "When shall we meet?" people say, "Between three o'clock and three thirty... maybe four o'clock."

We don't want that. We want to say, "It's either three o'clock or three thirty or four o'clock."

There can be constant shifts and changes in what you understand. You don't have to become uptight. It's not a matter of "This is *it*. This is what I said last year. This is what I'm saying now. This is what I'm going to say next year." No. As you grow, your understanding grows. Your understanding shifts. You become a better and better and better person.

When you are bringing up children, the most important thing is to love them. Even your anger has to be clouded with love. Don't just use anger to discipline them. Sometimes you can play with them. Or take a group and play with them. While you are all together, you can have a conversation. Whatever the issue is, they won't hold back. They will explain what they think: "No, no, it's not like that! It's like this!"

For example, I like to take a child for a walk around the ashram. During that walk, I find out many things.

Sometimes, even when I want to know about an adult, I go to the children. They will tell me exactly what happened between two adults. Clearly, without any filters. If one of the adults is there, that adult will definitely try to assert his views. But you know that the child has seen whatever took place and he will explain it to you correctly.

In our dealings with children, we have to remember that children at a young age have no axe to grind. For them, it is what it is. Only as we get older do we think we are so smart.

THE MOST AMAZING THING

Question: Why are we so afraid of dying if all we are doing is exchanging bodies? I mean, what's the big deal?

Gurudev: Until recently—and still a little bit—in India, you see death. When somebody dies, you see the body being carried out. You see the body going to the crematorium. There are twelve or thirteen days during which the families come together. People go and pay a visit to the family where the death has taken place. So death is constantly there. There is cause to be aware "I'm going to die."

But in modern society—for example, here in America—you would never know somebody has died, unless it was a neighbor or a family member. So you never ponder death. You never worry about death. You think you're going to live forever. As a matter of fact, advertisements promise you can live forever. As long as you get a face lift, you will always look young.

Four years ago, a woman we know died of cancer. The husband wanted the daughter, the son, myself, and the person who drove me there to watch the body being put into the oven.

The caretaker of the funeral home said, "I apologize that this doesn't look so good. Normally, it is just us. We take the casket from the front room, where everything looks beautiful, and bring it into the back and put it inside the oven." He said, "Until now, no family member has ever asked to see the oven into which the casket is put."

I was amazed because when my mother and father were cremated in India, the body was placed on top of a pyre. My youngest brother lit the fire, and we all stood there for a while and watched as the body burned. Some people waited for two or three hours.

All the cosmetic things we have done have taken death away from our eyes. As a result, we never think about death.

Actually, this is not just a problem today. Even in the *Mahābhārata*, Yudhiṣṭhira and all the disciples are asked, "What is it that is most amazing in this world?"

Yudhiṣṭhira answers, "The fact that somebody dies every

day, yet everyone acts as if he is immortal."
We think to ourselves, "I'm going to be around." So we are constantly collecting things, constantly gathering things, constantly accumulating things.

A swami shares a story. In it, a man goes to the Guru and says, "I have accumulated enough wealth for six generations. Now I'm worried about the seventh." He is old and doesn't have enough time to accumulate wealth for the seventh. He's not even going to be around to see the next generation enjoy what he has accumulated. And what about the other five? Yet this is how people live.

A fellow was here last night who has terminal cancer. He came up and said, "All these concepts I understand. I am aware of what death is and all that. But to actually feel it and experience it and live it..." He is young, under twenty-five.

We have to understand death from within ourselves. By hiding it, we don't really come to see it or experience it.

Of course, now there are classes on death and dying. They give lectures on death and dying. But the practical application we saw in India, at least growing up, we don't see anymore. You see a little bit here and there, but even in India now the body is often taken away in a hearse.

WE NEED TO DO MORE

Question: There is a lot of talk out there about the Age of Aquarius, higher Consciousness, and that sort of stuff. Can you touch on that?

Gurudev: According to Indian philosophy, we still have four hundred and twenty-some thousand years to go before we come into the Golden Age again. So it's not as bad yet as it's going to be.

I tell people who ask about this that there is really nothing to worry about.

People get so worked up about doomsday that they do crazy things. Of course, to them, it's a good way to make money because they can capitalize on people's fear. They say, "This is going to happen!" And people believe it.

Today, everybody has become a teacher. Everybody has become a knower of the Truth. Instead of only rare people teaching about the Truth, everybody wants to do it. I think there is nothing wrong with that. But both the student and the teacher have to know that what the teacher is teaching—and what the student is able to understand—is a small fraction of the actual Truth.

For example, sometimes people tell me they have written a book. If the original text that they wrote about was in Sanskrit, I ask, "How much of the Sanskrit do you know?"

They say, "Nothing."

"How could you write a book when the original was in Sanskrit?"

"Well, I took a few books that other people wrote, and I made up my own understanding of what they wrote."

"How do you know that what they wrote is true, is correct?"

"I don't know."

Or people read something they didn't hear about before and they think, "Wow!" Because they are enamored with it, they go and tell five of their friends. Those people didn't hear it before, either, and they go, "Wow!" They believe and trust the first person, so they take it as the ultimate Truth. And so it goes.

Today, with YouTube and Twitter and Google, you just have to put something out there, and if it goes viral, then it becomes the truth.

Question: I've noticed a shift. More people now are aware of energy, are doing yoga, being more positive. These people must have a tremendous effect on the world. Don't you think?

Gurudev: I don't find that, I'm sorry. I've been doing this work for fifty years now—thirty consciously, and about twenty years before that as a child. We read about yoga more in the media, but I don't necessarily think that means much. More people on the periphery may be enjoying yoga, but that doesn't mean more people are doing it today than were before.

Go to a shopping mall and see how many people are there shopping, and compare that with how many people are at a satsaṅg or a spiritual program. It's a small percentage, compared with the population of the world.

I may be wrong, but I think this is a realistic way to look at it.

When we traveled with Baba, sometimes five thousand people came to a program. I would think, "Five thousand people came to see my master. That's exciting!"

As I said last night, we think of Bhagavān Nityānanda sitting in the little village of Ganeshpuri, doing his meditation, his practice. He appears to be doing nothing, yet he is radiating energy. A sage or sādhu like that has an effect on fifty people, five hundred people, five thousand people—even without meeting them. But again, compare that with the population of the entire world.

We met Krishna Das a couple of years ago. He said he went to Brazil, and two hundred thousand people showed up at a kirtan.

The question is "What happened after the kirtan?" Whether it was five thousand people or fifty or a hundred or two hundred thousand, how many are conscious, are aware, and actually practice yoga? I would say a very small percentage.

Being here, it is easy to think, "I'm living in a peaceful, loving, joyous world." At the same time, so much else exists in this world.

When I first came to the United States in 1978, I learned that you didn't have to lock the doors here. You could leave things open and come back twenty-four hours later and still find your things lying there. Yesterday someone was saying that now she has to lock her car and lock her home. The country has changed. Of course, people always say, "Don't say negative things." But it's so.

How do we eradicate or eliminate these negative things? I think we are lazy. We don't do enough to make the world a more positive place.

How can all of us who have been awakened do more, radiate more?

Baba left his body in 1982. This year it will be thirty years. Sometimes I think about how much he did in just twelve years, in the time before he passed. I think, "What are we actually doing, compared with what he did?"

There is so much more that so many of us could do. We might have ten, twenty, thirty years of life left. What else can we do with what is left of our lives?

GURU AND DISCIPLE

Question: Would you speak on the role of the physical Guru?

Gurudev: Baba always said you learn everything in life from someone. So on the spiritual path, you also learn from someone.

I think you have to understand that relationship in the right way. Baba called it the perfect relationship.

First, be clear about who you are as a disciple. Second, be clear about who the Guru is. If you feel you want a Guru, or need a Guru, what are the qualities you are looking for?

I think this kind of understanding brings about a healthy relationship. Don't become fanatical. Just be clear, as you are clear about all relationships.

Question: Does the Guru choose the disciple, or does the disciple choose the Guru?

Gurudev: I think neither chooses the other. In my experience, it is a result of connections over lifetimes. It comes from a bond we have with a lineage or a tradition or a path.

In the sixth chapter of the *Bhagavad Gītā*, Kṛṣṇa explains that when you are doing yoga and you die, then you are reborn into a family who do yoga. And that leads you to the Guru.

The scriptures also give the example of a bee that goes from flower to flower to flower. When the bee finds a flower with the right nectar, it settles there. In the same way, a seeker goes here and there. But when the seeker finds the right Guru, and the right path with the right practices, he settles there.

Question: What made you become a swami? Was it a state of consciousness you reached? Or something you knew, a choice you made?

Gurudev: Well, first, I would say I had no choice. I think all of what has happened is the result of past life saṁskāras, of karmas, that come with one at birth.

As a young boy, I knew nothing about the Guru and disciple, about what that relationship is. There were no discussions about that. We didn't go to the ashram to hear Baba give talks. My mother simply told us, "He's God. You must do what he says."

That's all we knew.

So we grew up feeling a bond with Baba. At the same time, we were terrified of him. We were afraid of our mother and father, as well, but less so. Despite all that, there was an experience you could call bliss or love or joy. It was an experience that cannot be described in words.

When Baba took my sister Malti to be with him in August of 1973, I was ten years and some months old. I gathered the courage to ask my mother to let him know that I also wanted to join him.

I don't know exactly what my mother said because I wasn't present. But she came back and said, "Baba said boys have to live their own lives."

Of course, I was devastated. Nevertheless, I said to myself, "I can do that."

Some months later, I woke up one morning from a dream. I don't know how I still remember this, but I do. In the dream, I was about thirty-five years of age. I was sitting on the steps of a temple somewhere in India. I was dressed in orange, and I was doing japa with my mālā.

I woke up really surprised. I don't think I ever told anybody about that dream. They probably would have told me I was crazy.

After that, I just went about my life. I planned to become a mechanical engineer because that's where my interest lay.

In March of 1977, I finished my tenth-grade exams. Baba was staying in Mumbai. He had just gone through a heart attack and he was recuperating. I went every day to serve him. I was there from early morning until night.

One day, I walked into his room after darśan. I was going to put some stuff away there.

Baba was sitting on his bed. He said, "Hey!"

He never called me by my name. But at that moment I knew he was calling me. At first I kept walking, because I didn't want to talk to him. That could be risky. But when he said "hey" again, I knew I couldn't reach the door fast enough—it was a long walk from there to the door. So I turned around.

He said, "What are you going to do?"

I gave him a look that said, "Go outside."

But I knew, of course, exactly what he wanted to know. So we had a long conversation, and I told him what my plans were.

He said, "Very good."

We talked for forty-five minutes to an hour, and then I left.

A year later, on the 24th of April, at about eight o'clock in the evening, I went to the ashram to drop Malti off. The next day, I was going to take my exams at the institution known as IIP.

She said, "Come and say goodbye to Baba."

I said, "I already met him this morning. I don't need to disturb him now." I didn't know what the point of a conversation would be.

She said, "No, get his blessings."

I said, "He's already blessed me."

She insisted, so I went in.

Baba said, "Where are you going?"

I said, "I'm going to go take my exams for engineering college."

He said, "If you want to live with me, why do you want to become an engineer?"

I was totally aghast. Just a year and a few months before, we'd had a full-on conversation. I had been very clear about my plans, and he had given his blessing.

Now he said, "If you want to live with me, you should study philosophy."

In my mind, I recalled what my mother always said: "Never question Baba." The only thing we were taught to say was "*Ji*, Baba. Yes, Baba." So I said, "I will go to Bombay tomorrow morning."

The next day, I went to the college where I would have to apply to study philosophy.

The person said, "Come back in August."

Then I went to the teachers who had been helping me prepare for my engineering exam. I said, "I'm not going to do this exam." I told them not to ask why because I knew I would not be able to explain it to them.

I went back to the ashram and told Baba, "I have nothing to do till August."

He said, "Stay here with me."

And I'm still staying here with him. It is thirty-five years later, and of course a lot of things have happened. But that evening, on the 24th of April, was when the shift took place.

We had a few conversations along the way from that date until 1982. Baba was very abstract in his conversations—very to the point, but also abstract. When you were in front of him, you felt his energy; his powerful, dynamic presence. I never looked at him as I would look at someone in a normal conversation. I just looked down. I don't know how to begin to put into words what such a conversation was like. What words could convey the subtle electrical transmissions that took place?

For example, one time he said, "In three days you are going to take sannyāsa."

In that situation, do I say, "What do you mean?" Or do I just say okay?" Our modern mind would say, "Dialogue with him. Ask him. Talk to him."

But in my experience of growing up with Baba, that kind of dialogue did not exist. Also, somewhere deep within, I had the conviction and the understanding that there was no need for dialogue. Having had the realization that all of what was taking place is Consciousness—and that in that Consciousness, this play is taking place—I simply had to go with it.

The problem arises when you want to fix the play. You want to fine tune it, to adjust it. Often people ask, "How did this happen? Why did that happen?" They think, "I'm going to make this better."

You're wasting your time trying to figure out how or why it happened. It just happened. And you just go with it. You wake up each morning and you participate in the play. It's fun. You learn.

That is why I don't get excited about whether something is going to turn out well or poorly. It is what it is.

We learned around Baba to keep it dynamic. You keep it moving. You keep it exciting. You keep it fun. Shifts constantly take place within you. The ability to see is what is important. You see the subtle things that take place—that which is not seen by the eye, not understood by the mind. That is what is most exciting.

We celebrated Baba's hundredth birthday in the ashram in India. Some days into the celebration, I was sitting on my swing. Everybody was walking around. It was nine o'clock. I sensed that Baba was walking around too. It was a strong experience.

I paused for a moment and asked myself, "Are you imagining this? Is this in your mind?" But then, of course, I realized that, yes we were celebrating his birthday, so he was there celebrating with us.

We think to ourselves, "What is the Guru? What is Consciousness? What is God?" Often, we get caught in the words. At some point, you have to rise above that.

For instance, Baba was asked, "Do you see God in that tree?"

Baba said, "I see God as the tree."

We are trying to look for the divine. But the divine is always there.

Question: What role does the Guru in the physical sense play?

Gurudev: I just shared a little bit of that. First of all, there has to be a hundred percent trust between the Guru and the disciple. In Sanskrit there is a word, *śraddhā*. In English, I translate it as "faith without a question."

That faith can exist between a couple. It exists between a parent and a child. One has no doubt about the other. In the same way, that faith has to come about in the Guru-disciple relationship.

Baba told me, "You don't study engineering, you study philosophy." In that moment, there were so many questions I could have asked. I had spent three-and-a-half, four years preparing to be an engineer. I did three years of technical school, one year of science. And there was the tuition I had paid to prepare for the exam. Yet Baba was telling me, "Go and change all that."

Your faith can't just be on paper. Your entire being has to know that whatever happens will be fine, that it's what you want.

As soon as I followed Baba's command, I found out the philosophy program was not available until August. It was April 25, so what to do now? May, June, July: I had three-and-a-half months. So Baba said, "Stay here with me."

Shortly after that, one day I was bending down to pick up a basket of fruit. Baba turned to the person next to him and said, "Get him his passport. He's going to travel with me." That was in June.

I was about fifteen years and some months old. I didn't really know what traveling with Baba would mean. I saw that I was not going to college. I was not going to study. I was just going to be with Baba. But what was I going to do with him? The only useful things I could do were pick up the basket of fruit, sweep, mop—which I loved—and play the drums.

I didn't make friends in the ashram, except for a very few. It was clear to me that I was not there to be social. My relationship and bond were with Baba. He also made it clear in his own ways that I was to be there for him.

Within yourself as a disciple, you have to come to the understanding that you have a perfect relationship with the Guru. The Guru has already abandoned all individual feelings, thoughts, and experiences. So the Guru is ready to encompass everything and everybody.

Those who bonded with Baba in this way have found that his guidance and his grace are still with them. It's not that it only happened when he was alive, and now they have to wonder, "What do I do today?"

In 1986, I was staying with my parents. After a few months of not knowing what to do, I went to Bhagavān's samādhi shrine in Ganeshpuri. I sat there and sang *Āratī Karūṅ* in my head. I said, "Please, I need guidance. I need help. I need to know where my life is going. What am I going to do?"

I cried a lot there. It was not crying out of sadness or suffering or pain—just crying as a release of something. Then I went back to Bombay and told my mother, "On the 6th of October, my birthday, we will have satsaṅg."

She asked me again and again over the next few days, "You're sure you're going to have satsaṅg?" Because for the few months before that, I had told her very clearly, "I want nothing to do with yoga. I'm just going to live life."

Once she was convinced that I was speaking the truth, she organized a satsaṅg on my birthday. And that which began on October 6, 1986, we continue today.

That clarity has to come from within ourselves. It's not limited to a communication from the physical Guru. It's an energy that exists. What we know as the Guru comes through a particular embodiment at different times.

Each of us, in our life, may connect with such a being at some point.

There have been many, many, many, teachers. But I think such Gurus—whom you could call live wires, who can give so much and have such intensity—are rare. If you just think of them, let alone be in their presence, things happen that you can hardly imagine.

All these things you read and hear about are true. But again, you have to be ready in that moment to perceive it. You have to be willing to take it in.

Swami Rām Tīrth sings a poem: "O Lord, what is it that I have not gotten from you? What is it that I cannot ask of you?

It is just that my bag is small and I cannot take everything you are willing to give."

This is what often happens. You go to such a Guru and say, "I want A. I want B. I want C. I want D. I want E."

He says, "Okay. I want to give you F, G, H, I, J, K, L, M, N, O, P, Q, R."

You say, "Wait, no, no. I just want A to E."

So you get A to E. Then you read in a book that you can get A to Z. And you say, "But I only got A to E!"

You forget you were the one who bargained for A to E, and said wait for the F to Z. You compare notes with somebody else: "You got A to Z? How come I only got A to E?" Well, that is what you bargained for when you went to him.

I always say, "When you pray, just pray." Don't make a deal. Don't say, "I want this or I want that." Just pray, and that which is yours will come to you.

It has been thirty years since Baba took samādhi. I have traveled the world a lot in these thirty years. I've met many kinds of people. There are wonderful people; really great, great, —people—whether swamis of the Indian tradition or teachers of other traditions. But I have not come across a being like Baba. Such ones, who can constantly pulsate with the Truth, are rare.

All of that which I am is because of him. I wouldn't be here doing this today. I'd probably be working on a factory floor or at a design table, drawing something. Or jobless, who knows? All that has happened is because of that one moment in his room, when my life was transformed.

Yet if we think, what was that moment? It was not that one moment, but it was a moment that sparked so many moments.

MAKE THE MIND YOUR SERVANT

Question: Does the mind itself progress on the path? Or does your mind still give you so much trouble even as you advance on the path?

Gurudev: We can begin with what the *Upaniṣads* say: "We are what we eat." We start with food because that is what, on the most gross level, can affect the mind. If you become conscious of what you put into your body, you will see that this in itself can create a shift.

For example, as I travel, many people ask me why I don't eat onions and garlic.

I say, "In 1990, I took an initiation that prohibited onions and garlic." Before that, in Baba's ashrams, most of the recipes had onions and garlic, so we ate lots of onions and garlic. Maybe eight or ten years after the initiation, I became aware that a shift had taken place. Of course, whether it was the rest of the practice I do or the removal of onions and garlic that caused the shift is hard to say.

Many traditions, in India anyway, eliminate onions and garlic as part of their spiritual practice. I don't know what scientists say, but spiritual practitioners agree that onions can cause excitement in the mind and body.

As a seeker, if you become aware that your mind is bothering you, you can go through a process of identifying and eliminating those foods that are the cause. Over time, your awareness becomes subtle enough to know what is affecting you. And you develop discipline and control over what you eat.

For example, I love chocolate, but I can't eat too much of it because I know what it does to me. At some point, I have to tell myself, "Stop." I know I don't want to eat the whole bar.

Second, the company you keep.

You might think, "Everybody is Consciousness. Everybody is God. Everybody is good." Yes. But everybody also vibrates at a different level. When you become aware that a particular friendship, relationship, or discussion is not going anywhere, you have to be smart. It may be difficult, but you learn when it's time to simply say, "Bye-bye."

Become free of the things you read that are not uplifting. Become free of the things you listen to that are not uplifting. Become free of TV shows that are not good. Become free of movies that are not good. Each of these things leaves an imprint on the mind.

When you go through a process of elimination, you find, "Okay, there are still a few things that are good, that work for me." You rely and depend upon those things. And then slowly you free yourself from even those things. Instead of depending on them, they are just there to enjoy when you want.

In answer to your question, as you progress, your mind progresses too. You learn to see the mind as your servant.

Right now, you may be the servant of your mind. Your mind says, "Get up." And you get up. Your mind says, "Don't get up." And you don't get up. Right?

If you feel that you want to leave a space, you should have the strength within yourself to say, "Okay, I'm going to leave now."

The mind may give all its arguments and counter arguments about why you should do something or why not. But be clear in your mind about what you want.

Baba used to say, "You are what you think."

So the quality of your thoughts has to change.

Why do people do silly things? Because their mind makes them do silly things. When people don't do silly things, it doesn't necessarily mean they don't have silly thoughts. But they have gotten control over themselves. They say, "That's a silly idea. I won't do it." Eventually, they reach a point where they no longer have those thoughts.

Question: If we are just beginning on this path, what would you suggest we read?

Gurudev: There is a book in the bookstore called *Conversations with Swami Muktananda*. There is one copy left because

I took the other copy the other day.

It is questions and answers with Baba from the sixties. The answers are very candid because Baba shares his thoughts freely.

As you go on, you will find many books. However, be careful and conscious not to get caught up in too many books and too many words. You can get lost in the words.

I have found over the years that the best way is to read and then try to practice those teachings. If you don't understand them, read them again. There's nothing wrong with that. Try again. Go a little further. Stop. It's not like a novel that you read in one sitting. Well, you could do that because there is a lot of energy and excitement. But to really digest and imbibe what Baba talks about is a slow process.

I think of yoga as a process of simmering. To stay with it for the long haul, you have to go slowly. You can't rush and think you have got it all overnight.

Some people say they woke up one morning and got it all. That is the best lie I've ever heard.

We have a mind. We have a brain. We have an intellect. These faculties need to understand what is happening.

The sages who sit and meditate and contemplate are not fools. They go through the whole process. Only then do they share their process and understanding with us.

So go slowly. Do your practice regularly, every single day. And the illuminations that are meant to happen will happen.

Question: Is it necessary to read the commentary on a sūtra? Sometimes there are twenty pages of commentary, and I find that just makes me confused.

Gurudev: If you understand the sūtra, then you don't need the commentary. If you don't understand the sūtra, then you need the commentary.

INTENSITY OF PRACTICE

Question: When I meditate, I don't seem to go beyond a certain level. Do I keep on doing what I'm doing, or is there anything else I can do?

Gurudev: You have to improve what you are doing.

Ask yourself, "Am I actually doing the best I can? Are my efforts a hundred percent?"

As we read in Baba's *Reflections of the Self*, don't be lethargic.

Often we say, "I do japa." But what happens if you take a mālā and keep count, and then ask yourself, "Was I aware of all the 108 times I did japa?" How many times did you go to a thought, get lost, and then come back?

This kind of analysis can only be done by you.

Or when you sit to meditate, how many minutes of the hour that you sat were in actual stillness, quiet, emptiness? How many minutes were in thoughts, dreams, sleep?

Similarly, when you chant. For example, the *Guru Gītā* has 182 verses. Ask yourself, "How many of those 182 verses did I really chant? For how many verses did I go to Mexico or to India or to a conversation?"

Kabīr says that it is our intensity that is doing the work. In his poem, he speaks of being a "slave of intensity."

When I think now of living with Baba, the best part—though we didn't understand it at the time—was his intensity. For all of us who got somewhere in those years, it was intense. But that intensity is what has borne fruit.

Look at people who have gotten somewhere in life. They are all intense people. Their intensity has gotten them where they are.

If you think you can't get to the next level in meditation, that means your intensity has to increase. Nobody can increase that intensity except you. That intensity is within, not on the outside.

We always think, "I am doing a lot." But then we see somebody who is doing more. Recently, I mentioned to somebody that I feel I am not doing much.

She said, "How can you say that?"

I said, "Well, I compare myself with Baba." He was much older physically than I am now, so I consider how much he did even at that age.

I won't become intense now. That's one good thing! But your practices have to become intense.

THE BREATH

Question: Sometimes I can't meditate, no matter how hard I try. Is there anything I can do to help myself focus and concentrate?

Gurudev: I think you can do two things: one is prāṇāyāma and one is japa. These are the best ways to quiet an agitated mind. But most importantly, I would say you have to become aware of why your mind becomes like that.

Of course, all minds go to those places you are talking about.

When people are young, they tend to worry a lot. Hopefully, as you get older and wiser, you don't allow the mind to remain tense or agitated. You understand that worrying doesn't get you anywhere.

Sometimes I suggest people listen to the mantra *Oṁ Namaḥ Śivāya* playing through a computer or speakers in some form. That way, it can be louder than your thoughts. Because your thoughts are so loud, you have to physically force the mantra to penetrate them.

Sometimes it's a war. The mind says, "I don't want to listen anymore."

Then you have to stop the mantra for a moment. Understand that it's just energy within you that needs release. So you find different ways to release that energy.

Maybe do some hatha yoga. Or take a walk. Look at the trees. Look at the sky. There's nothing like nature. It allows you to become connected within yourself.

You can practice various types of prāṇāyāma. Don't try to do three or four ways at one time. You have to make a choice. Of course, the most basic one, deep yogic breathing, is something we do at all times.

Bhastrikā is good because it's forceful. It brings you to a place where you have retention of breath, kumbhaka. When kumbhaka occurs, you experience inner quietness or stillness of mind.

I wouldn't say you will necessarily reach a hundred percent thought-free state. Thoughts will still be there. It's like shaking out a rug. When you shake a rug, all the dust flies around. You have to take the rug away before the dust settles back into it.

In the same way, you can think of prāṇāyāma as a shaking away of thoughts. It is a loosening up, a letting go of habitual thoughts. Otherwise, as you continually sit with your thoughts, they eat you up.

As you get wiser, you no longer choose to sit with those thoughts. You learn to walk away. So find the technique that works best for you, whether it's prāṇāyāma, japa, listening to the mantra, or something else.

One good habit is to read a good book, such as a book with stories about the great beings. However, when your mind is agitated, it may reject this. It may tell you, "No, I don't want to read that."

In this case, you have to force yourself to read it. Tell your mind, "Yes! This is where I want to be."

It's like scrubbing a brass pot. Slowly it does begin to shine. It has been tarnished for some time, so you need to keep rubbing it. The mind is the same way. It's tarnished, or agitated, with its own thoughts. Whichever polishing method you find that works is what you have to do. And stick with it.

Question: What are the various different prāṇāyāmas? What do you teach about them?

Gurudev: There are many different kinds of prāṇāyāma. You can do them before meditation.

Bhastrikā is the bellows breath, breathing rapidly in and out. *Ujjāyī* has a forced out-breath, with a natural in-breath. And there is the simple prāṇāyāma, where you hold one nostril closed as you take the breath in. Then you switch sides and let the breath out through the other nostril.

There are rules and regulations with prāṇāyāma. For example, you cannot do it until two hours after you have eaten. You cannot eat for one hour after you've done prāṇāyāma.

When you do prāṇāyāma wisely and well, it affects the entire body, not just the lungs or the diaphragm or the abdomen. You want to do it so well that the energy flows and moves throughout the body.

To get the best effect, you should learn it from a good teacher. Practice it well, and then it bears fruit.

FILLED WITH LIGHT

Question: The other day you said that it is very easy to see the light. But it's also very easy to see the darkness. How do you distinguish?

Gurudev: We are taught about the importance of company. Depending on the company you keep, you will experience either light or darkness. So we're taught to always keep good company.

Different people have said that the sign of the touch of God's hand is that what was unreal in their life begins to drop away. For years, they were fine with all those things in their life. But then as they became filled with light and joy, that was what they wanted to surround themselves with.

As you become filled with light and joy, you automatically draw that toward yourself. Darkness will also come. In the same way that a flat tire or a pothole or a traffic jam are inevitable, darkness will appear.

In that moment, you have two choices. On the one hand, if you are able and strong enough, share the light with others. On the other hand, if you feel unable to share the light or if the other person is unwilling—which sometimes happens—you simply have to let it go.

It doesn't make sense to become dark yourself in an attempt to bring light to someone else. Then you have lost your own purpose. Only if you stay lit can you continue to share your light with another person. Even if the person doesn't see the light in that moment, if you keep walking, at some point he or she will catch up with you and say, "I now understand what you said then."

Nothing appears clear to us when we are not saturated with light.

You take pictures with a camera. If you think back to when you started, you always needed a light meter to tell you how much light there was. Now, after years of experience, you have a general idea of what it is. The meter only seconds what you think.

In the same way, in life, in the beginning we don't really recognize what is light and what is darkness. But after we have put in the time and done the practice, we are able to walk into any space and immediately know what is happening in that space.

Part of a priest's job is to bring light wherever he goes. In return, he receives gifts and money. But people also give their darkness or their pain through those gifts. The transfer that takes place is not physical. Yet the priest has to know how to cleanse himself with mantras and other practices when he gets home.

You may think it's not so easy to see the light. But that is only a result of living in darkness. When you come to light, you realize darkness is not as enjoyable or fulfilling as light is.

As we travel the world, all kinds of people come to our programs. Some come and cry. Usually the crying is out of joy. But it can also be a release of the darkness, pain, and suffering they have been going through. They realize, "My life can be full of light and joy. There is no need to be in darkness."

That is what I wish and pray is the outcome of every program.

If you go to the shrines of great saints, you will find that the vibration in that place is still strong today, even centuries after they lived there.

Last year, we went to a deserted place in Spain. The person who took us said a monastery stood in that spot a few hundred years ago, and a saint lived there. A little chapel is still standing. It was locked up, but sometimes people go there to pray. A few hundred feet down, we saw water flowing. And birds flying through the forest. We could feel what it must have been like years ago when the saint and his disciples lived there. If we could feel that now, just think how it must have been when they were actually doing what they were doing.

That's why I say each of us has to create a lifestyle that is full of light and joy. Then when people come into our home or our workspace, that's what they will feel and experience.

Some people tell me I should come to their home every year. I ask them why.

"Because," they say, "before you come, the whole house gets cleaned." And they say, "At least then we know once a year our house will be clean."

People who like food say, "My wife and my mother-in-law will cook good food."

The truth is, all of us like light. The sages tell us that it is the nature of every individual to love light.

Whenever we feel pain or suffering, we run to where we know we can get love. That love is like a cocoon, and we forget our pain and suffering.

Devayani used to love visiting her grandmother. There was a three-person sofa, and a La-Z-Boy on the side where her grandfather sat. The grandmother sat in one corner of the sofa, and the other two spaces were taken by Devayani as she lay in her grandmother's lap. The grandmother was eighty-something, and Devayani was thirty-something. The grandmother would run her fingers through Devayani's hair. The grandfather on his La-Z-Boy said, "You're a woman now, not a baby!"

Age does not matter. It does not matter in giving, and it does not matter in receiving. As humans, we have to learn to give and receive. Sometimes we have a problem with both. We don't know how to give, and we don't know how to receive.

One of the teachings of Bhagavān Nityānanda was viśala hṛdaya. Have a big heart.

Imagine what big must have meant to him. He lay there on his little blanket on a piece of stone. In the pictures, you can see the piles of fruit and flowers and cloth and coconuts all around. And he just lay there in his own bliss. Somebody who wanted a coconut took a coconut. Somebody who wanted a flower took a flower. To him, it didn't matter.

His best friends were little kids. He had the most fun with them.

So learn to give. When something comes, be able to receive it also. Don't say "I only give." Or "I only receive." The way it works is that what comes around goes around. If you think, "I want love," start by giving love. As soon as you start giving, you will see there are so many piles around you. Because what do the coconuts, flowers, and cloth represent? They represent love.

We don't give. And then we say, "I don't get anything." So start giving. You could start right now, but I think everybody here is already saturated. So start as soon as you get home. A few months ago somebody sent me a joke. A man went home from satsaṅg. He picked his wife up and started dancing around the house.

She said, "What did Swamiji say at satsaṅg today?"

He said, "To carry your problems with great love and joy."

Question: Is chanting equal to meditation? Chanting makes me full, but I meditate very little.

Gurudev: I think we must chant a lot. Just as the man in that joke carried his wife, we must carry ourselves with great love and joy.

We've just come from Argentina, where they tango. They tango during chanting too. The way they chant is so passionate. Wherever we go now, I think we can measure our chanting based upon what we experienced in Argentina. In most countries around the world, I find people are very reserved, very shy.

The way to chant is to become immersed in the chant. When you chant well, the result is natural meditation.

It is good to find time every day to sit.

It's not necessary to say to yourself, "I'm going to meditate." Because you can't actually say, "I'm going to meditate." Meditation is the natural outcome of what you do.

Throughout the day, you have to be conscious in everything you do. Therefore, in the morning, you sit to prepare yourself for the day.

If during the day you feel distracted, take a few moments to breathe, to be quiet. Then at the end of the day, as you lie down to go to sleep, become still and quiet again.

Some people tell me they can drink a cup of coffee and it

won't have any effect. But unless you have experienced a quiet mind, you don't know what a quiet mind is. Once you have experienced a quiet mind, you will never enjoy a non-quiet mind.

The whole process of prāṇāyāma and meditation brings you to a place of stillness. Once you have experienced that stillness, you don't really enjoy anything else.

You probably don't realize that you sat for almost two hours and twenty minutes this morning. They say the typical sustained attention span nowadays is about twenty minutes. So to have sat quietly in one place for as long as you did is an achievement in itself. You didn't think, "I'm going to the bathroom." You didn't think of your phone. You didn't think of whatever else you naturally do when "it's been fifteen minutes."

Baba once told me, "People are all different. Some will love meditation. Some will love chanting. Some will love reading. Some people like to work." He said, depending on their preferences, people will do more of whatever they like.

I still think you must find time each day to simply sit, be still, be quiet. It doesn't have to be a set time—such as fifteen minutes, thirty minutes, or one hour—but just a period to assess what is going on within yourself.

There is a Sanskrit word, *svādhyāya*. *Sva* means self. *Adhyāya* means chapter or study. That means each day we must do self-study. We must ask ourselves, "Where am I today?"

I'd like to leave you with this thought. When you go home, create a schedule for yourself. Try to follow it every single day. That way, you will not miss your daily practice of svādhyāya.

If you go to our website, you'll see that each of our ashrams has a daily schedule. For us, that's great. Each day when we wake up, we know what will happen throughout the day. Meditation and chanting are interspersed with other activities.

If you follow a schedule for svādhyāya, then even if darkness comes to you, you will be forced to see the light. As you chant and as you keep the company of fellow seekers, at some point you will face yourself.

THE CYCLE OF REINCARNATION

Question: I believe that we come from God and our soul is part of that divinity. If our soul is part of that divinity, why do we have to reincarnate to learn in this life?

Gurudev: The divine exists within each one of us. Even though it exists within us, few of us accept the existence of that divinity. No matter how much we read and know and accept and understand, we live in ignorance of that fact.

We worship sages and saints because they have reached a point where they can say, "I am divine." In that experience, they do not think, "I am doing this." Rather, they are aware that they are an instrument through whom the divine is acting.

When you come to that understanding, then the cycle of reincarnation ends. Until such a time, you feel "I am doing all this," and the whole process of karma is active. The world goes on. There is creation, sustenance, dissolution.

Most of you in Mexico have probably seen two pieces of stone between which some kind of grain is put and is ground into flour.

As the story goes, the poet-saint Kabīr is watching a woman grind flour. He sees the grain go into the stones and come out as flour. He sits there crying.

A sage comes by and asks, "Kabīr, why are you crying?"

Kabīr says, "This stone is like the wheel of time. Everyone who goes through is ground and becomes flour. Therefore, I am thinking to myself that I also will be ground by the wheel of time."

The woman uses a stick to push the grain between the stones. The sage takes this stick and shows Kabīr that a few grains are still stuck to it. They have not been ground. So the sage says, "Hold onto the divine, and you won't be ground up."

This is what the sages have been able to do. Divinity is not just a concept in their minds. Having become aware of their own divinity, they hold onto it. When you also learn this, you won't be ground in the cycle of reincarnation.

Question: When people talk about karma, usually it has a negative connotation. At what point can one begin to create only good karma?

Gurudev: I always begin by saying the subject of karma is very complex. If you talk about it one way, immediately the mind has other questions. I'll share a story one of Baba's swamis used to tell. It expresses well how karma works.

Satsaṅgs like this one used to happen around Baba a lot. The meditation hall had doors that would open, and then they would close as you walked in. One day, a person was walking out the door. The person in front of him let go of the door, and so his fingers got caught. Of course, his fingers were hurt. He began to get angry. He thought to himself, "That person was planning this for so many days." And he began to think to himself what he could do to take revenge on that person.

In the evenings after satsaṅg, we would all go to dinner. Just as we do here, we had a dining hall. The dinner usually was soup, salad, and bread.

As the person went for dinner, he was still lost in his thoughts about his fingers, about the one who let the door go, about planning revenge. He took his tray and his bowl. He walked through the line, and the server put soup in his bowl. He kept walking and thinking, not looking to see what was happening ahead of him. Of course, the person ahead of him stopped to take bread and salad. So he bumped into that person. His hot soup flew all over. He thought, "Today is a bad evening! My karma is horrible!"

The swami would say, "Stop here for a moment." He would retrace the steps: "The soup goes back in the bowl. The soup goes back in the pot. The person goes back to satsaṅg." He said, "Eventually you come back to the moment the door hit his fingers."

In that moment, he said, the person has a choice. He can simply look at his fingers and say, "Oh, my karma is being worked out." He can get some ice or some ointment. He doesn't have to think that the other person was planning this. He doesn't have to get angry or upset. He doesn't have to have a reaction.

In this case, we would say he is becoming free of *prārabdha* karma, the karma that has been allotted to him in this lifetime. By not reacting or getting upset or wanting to take revenge, he is not creating more karma for the future. Whatever had to be worked out is worked out. The whole cycle ends right there, right in that moment.

I will tell you that this is not so easy. Don't worry that from tomorrow on, you will never react. But you will have the wisdom to react less, or to get over your reaction more quickly. That wisdom will dawn within you.

This is why I say, "We take yoga with us everywhere."

Last year a woman spent a month in silence. At the end of the month, somebody asked her, "What did you learn from being silent?"

She said, "I learned I don't have to answer right away, that I can take a moment to think before I answer."

When you are in silence—unless you carry a pen and paper—what are you going to say? And if you do use a pen and paper, you are not really staying in silence.

Sometimes in the ashram people wear a badge: "I am in silence." I think if you are in silence, you are in silence. Why do you have to advertise that you are in silence? That means your silence is simply for the world outside, and you are just as much at work on the inside.

Usually when somebody gets into a negative space, that person gathers around friends who also are in a negative space. They all discuss how horrible everything is. By the same token, when you are in a good mood, you seek out friends who are in a good mood. Together, you discuss how good the world is. You all agree, "Yes, it is a wonderful place."

Somebody came up earlier and said, "How do I carry the sensation I've had in the last twenty-four hours constantly?"

You simply learn to carry it. The way you feel now is how

you should feel always. Why should you feel any different? We aren't really doing anything so special. We are simply in good company. We are with wonderful people. Everybody is mostly happy. We are chanting. We are meditating. We are talking about the good and the wonderful things life has to give all of us.

There's a school of yoga in Adelaide, Australia. Once every three months or so, they invite everybody from the city for kirtan. They have maybe five hours of kirtan, and then they serve soup and bread and whatever the community has prepared. Even those who do not do yoga come because they think, "At least it feels good. And at the end, you get soup and bread."

Even if somebody is afraid of yoga, that person will eat. When he eats food that has been prepared while people are chanting, the śakti will go inside him.

Baba always said this is the best way to reach a person. He said, "While you cook, chant." In that way, the mantra goes into the food.

The sages found wonderful ways to inject us with śakti. We don't even know when we have been injected. Yet as we think about it, we realize we are content. We enjoy that we have been injected.

So I suggest you get together and have kirtan.

About five hundred years ago, a saint named Chaitanya Mahāprabhu lived in Bengal, India. The Hare Kṛṣṇa tradition came from there. He and a few of his disciples would walk through the streets chanting, "*Hare Kṛṣṇa, Hare Kṛṣṇa, Hare Kṛṣṇa!*"

No matter who came into that energy field, the person was transformed by the śakti of that kirtan. It is said that thieves and robbers and their cohorts came. Caitanya Mahāprabhu simply hugged them. Prostitutes came, and he hugged them. Simply being in that environment caused a transformation. People forgot who they were, what they were. They would join in, "*Hare Kṛṣṇa, Hare Kṛṣṇa!*"

For this reason, we are always grateful to the Guru for the

grace, the knowledge, and the wisdom he has given us.

We may not always understand the depth of what we have received. But a seed has been planted within us. Through lifetimes, it bears fruit. All we have to learn is to enjoy the fruits of that which we have been given.

All over the world, I can guarantee there is no feeling that tops how we feel now. It is a feeling that is true. It arises from within ourselves. It is not dependent on anything outside.

You can call it *ānanda*, or bliss. You can call it peace. You can call it Consciousness. You can call it divine.

Kabīr says, "You can give a mute person dulce de leche and ask him, 'How does it taste?' But he doesn't have any words to describe it because he can't speak." Kabīr says the experience we have is like that. We are mute because we have no words to express the bliss we feel.

Just allow yourself to go into that space. It will always be there. Remember that, and keep it alive.

Question: How can I resolve my karma in this life?

Gurudev: How old are you?

Question: Thirteen.

Gurudev: That's good. At least at thirteen you are asking yourself this question.

Our scriptures tell us there are three kinds of karma. There is that which you have done before, which has accumulated over lifetimes. Some of this *sañcita* karma has been allotted to be used up in this lifetime. As you go through this lifetime, you create more karma through your actions and reactions. That is prārabdha karma, which then goes back into the accumulated karma.

The swami who taught me this when I was sixteen explained it very simply. He said, "Think of sañcita karma as a savings account. You don't really touch it. It's there for use when you need it. In the meantime, it's just sitting there earning interest. Prārabdha, or what is current, is like a checking account. You use it as you need it. And then there is *kriyamaṇa*, or future, karma, which is like the paycheck you get from your work."

When you understand karma in this way, you see that you have to be very conscious as you live life.

Whenever something happens, it may seem natural to have a reaction. But the point you want to come to is not to have that reaction. As soon as you react, you create an opposite reaction in the other person with whom the karma is taking place. Instead, realize that whatever is happening now is the outcome of what you did previously.

There is a great story that I often share that illustrates what would happen if we all come to that realization.

Two monks live together. They lead a very peaceful, wonderful life.

The younger monk tells the older monk one day, "We should be normal."

The older monk says, "How is that?"

The younger monk says, "We should fight."

The older monk says, "How would we fight?"

The younger monk says, "Here is a piece of gold. I'll put it between the two of us. I'll say it's mine. You say it's yours. I'll say it's mine; you say it's yours. We'll have a fight."

The older monk says, "Okay." He says, "This is mine."

The younger one says, "No, it is mine."

The older monk says, "No, it is mine."

The younger one, "No! It is mine."

The older one says, "If it's yours, then take it."

Imagine if we all could live life in this way. Whatever comes we accept. Whatever goes we accept also. We accept it as part of the cycle of life.

We accept with great joy when a child is born. We all celebrate; we have a big party. Imagine if the same child dies in a few days. We don't have a party. We have a long face, red eyes. We complain to God. All the joy is gone.

Instead, we can realize and remember that this is simply a cycle of life. If something has come, at some point it will go. And if it goes, at some point it will come back. Therefore, like the older monk, we must say, "If it is yours, have it."

Don't choose when and how and where you will follow this teaching. It must be consistent, twenty-four hours a day, in all actions, in all thoughts, in all speech. The sense of detachment must be there with everything that happens in life.

The *Upaniṣads* say, "Enjoy life, but without attachment."

When the sense of doership does not exist anymore, no karma is created for the future. If all of us could learn this, life would be wonderful. The whole cycle of karma would come to an end.

Our scriptures tell us that our old, accumulated karma is burned in the fire of knowledge, of wisdom. Roasted seeds do not sprout. This is a state of mind, of awareness, we have to come to within ourselves. When we come to that place, we are free of karma.

Question: Could you talk a little bit more about karma and free will?

Gurudev: Suppose somebody says something or does something that is not nice. At that point, what people normally do is just punch back. But, you have a choice in the moment to say instead, "Okay, that's fine. That was just the result of a past-life karma" and walk on. This is free will.

It's an interesting subject, one you can talk a lot about. But really, you can only go so far with all the theories. At a certain point, you have to say, "Let it be so."

If you are wondering, "What did I do first to create the bad karma I'm suffering today?" you're going to have to go to a psychic to get the answer. And then the psychic will tell you this and that, and you'll get caught in all of this and all of that.

People ask me, "What do you think of astrology?"

I always remember what an astrologer told me. He said, "I

view astrology like a weather report. You look at the report and know whether you should take your raincoat and umbrella, or whether you should take your jacket, or whether it's going to be warm and sunny."

That's how I view astrology. It helps you understand what is happening. It's not that you live by it, but you take it for what it is.

Don't drive yourself nuts trying to understand it all. Until one gets to the ultimate state, no one can understand it all. There are always little loopholes in everything. That's the way God made it. It is that wanting to know that keeps you on the edge, that keeps you going. You feel you've got to find the answer to that one thing, and then everything will make sense. But then when you find the answer to that one thing, you have yet another new thing to understand.

BECOME A GOPĪ

Question: I would like to know more about love, and Kṛṣṇa and the *gopīs'* love.

Gurudev: I often talk about this, and it's an hour-long talk. But we don't have that long now.

To understand gopī *bhāva*, you have to become like the gopīs. In that love, there cannot be any petty attachments or petty needs. Your smallness has to go away. Your love has to become such that there is no want in it.

A gopī doesn't see duality, doesn't see separation.

When we think of a great sage and what that sage did in his life, we would have to say he was like a gopī. The sage forgot everything on a personal level and simply shared his love, his goodness.

If we worship and honor a sage, in any tradition, what we are really worshipping is his love. That love is all that each and every one of us wants.

If you take a cat on your lap, the cat purrs. I'm not a big fan of cats, but I love the sound a cat makes when you pet it the right way. A dog, of course, puts its four legs up and totally surrenders himself. You know he is absorbing your love. What humans do, I don't know. Yet I would say that when we get that purity of love, an experience takes place.

When Kṛṣṇa sent Uddhava to teach the gopīs about meditation, Uddhava found them all running around, hugging cows, hugging trees, hugging each other. In each other and every thing, all they saw was Kṛṣṇa.

Uddhava thought, "The Lord has sent me to fix the right people." He proceeded to give them a lecture. He instructed them to sit in one place, close their eyes, turn within, and find Kṛṣṇa.

The gopīs said, "Why should we close our eyes? Why should we sit in one place to look for Kṛṣṇa, when everywhere we look and everything and everybody we see is Kṛṣṇa?"

Ask yourself this question: "How do I bring myself to that place where I see everything and everybody—good or bad, it doesn't matter—as divine, as the Self, as Consciousness?"

I love the story of Caitanya Mahāprabhu. It is said that all he did was chant. At first, it was just he and his friend and disciple, Nityānanda. Then others came. At some point, robbers joined him. Prostitutes joined him. Different kinds of people joined him. He would simply hug or touch them, and they would enter into that space where chanting was happening.

So wherever you are—at home, in your workplace, or anywhere you go—you can become a gopī. You can become a Caitanya Mahāprabhu. You can become a Baba. I don't necessarily mean in the way you look or talk or dress, but in your attitude, your behavior, your dealings, your thoughts, your speech. Then, when people feel the space you have created, they go, "Wow!"

If you think about the time from whenever you met Baba until now, there have been so many golden moments. We have all had many gopī moments. We have had many Caitanya Mahāprabhu moments.

The question is, "How do you keep that moment going so it is not just a moment recorded at some point in time?"

You can't just say, "I had two years with Baba." You have to think about how you can make that experience constant. How do you become unselfish? How do you become loving at all times? How can you be kind at all times? How can you be fun to be around at all times?

These are all qualities that the daily schedule around Baba invoked. We got up in the morning, and there was excitement about going to the temple. There was excitement about going to chant. There was excitement about going to do sevā, to your work. There was excitement about going to the meal. In Ganeshpuri, the food might not have been exciting, but there was still excitement. You would see Baba. You would experience the ashram life. And there was excitement again in the afternoon, and in the evening. You went to sleep. Even though you knew you would only get four or five hours of sleep, you were excited to wake up the next morning.

Ask yourself now, "What was it?"

I don't think we can say there was any one particular thing that made us excited. The whole quality of life was exciting. I think that's what you have to find even now. You have to get excited.

When you think about wanting to understand Kṛṣṇa and the gopīs, you have to go deep within yourself to that place where the experience is amazing, wonderful, filled with excitement.

THE LIGHT OF MANY BULBS

Question: What is the value of chanting in a group?

Gurudev: You feel support from everybody else. When people have a drink, they don't drink by themselves. They go somewhere where everybody else is drinking. It's more fun that way. Similarly, when you chant, it is more fun to chant with others.

Of course, occasionally it's fun to chant by yourself. But the energy of many people coming together to chant is very powerful. One bulb by itself would not give very much light in this room. But sixteen bulbs in this room give a lot of light.

Question: My way of participating in the Navrātra chant is just to absorb the energy, the sound, the rhythm, the dynamics. Is that okay?

Gurudev: That's what we did around Baba when we sat with the Brahmins. They chanted, and we followed the rhythm of their chanting. We had no books. But their whole purpose was to invoke that energy within us.

In Shaivism, *mātṛkā* śakti is the principle that describes how sound vibrates within the body. The energy affects many different things within us.

We perform this worship of the Devī externally only because the rituals are visually beautiful and draw the mind. Then we do what is called *aṅga-nyāsa* and *kara-nyāsa*. We imagine that we are the deity, and we use each syllable of the mantra to invoke the deity within our body. In this way, we start out with external worship and slowly we internalize it.

As humans with minds and egos, we want to understand everything. But if you look at the life you have lived for so many years, how much do you really understand? For example, how do you go to sleep? What is the actual process that happens when you fall asleep? What is it that wakes you up in the morning?

We have been sleeping since we were little ones, and we still don't know how we sleep. If we don't understand so many matters related to the body, how can we begin to comprehend what the sages are trying to tell us?

At the same time, I think that as we chant, and as we surrender, knowledge comes of its own accord. The knowledge the sages expressed came from within them. That knowledge also exists within us.

When you try to understand why, for example, the Goddess is holding a sword or a lotus, you might get one explanation from one person and a different explanation from someone else. Then you become confused about what is true. But when you go within and find the experience within yourself, you are able to feel what is true for you.

In the early days around Baba, nothing was really explained. Yet people had very profound and powerful experiences. They may not have understood it at the time, but at some point, the meaning became clear. The same thing happens with worship. In the beginning, you may not understand it fully, but it becomes clearer as you go along.

Question: As you are chanting the *Lalitā Sahasranāma*, is the meaning it conveys in your mind?

Gurudev: With some verses, yes. It is a very long chant. At the moment, we only chant it for nine days twice a year, during Navrātra. Then we put it away.

I don't try to visualize what I'm chanting. It's more a matter of internalizing it.

I sometimes wonder why I am interested in this chant. It is not something we learned from Baba. He never talked about it, except when the priests performed the Caṇḍī yajña in Ganeshpuri a few times over the years. But there was a natural interest that took me to Śrī Chakra and to Devī worship. Now we've done it for some time.

When I first started, I didn't know why, other than that I was drawn.

With any spiritual path, you have to be drawn. Then, as you

do the practices, you begin to develop interest. As that takes place, what was already within you is awakened or enlivened. Knowledge of your past experiences comes to light and illumines what you may not yet have understood.

When I first read the *Lalitā Sahasranāma*, some things immediately made sense, and other things I had to read carefully to understand. Sometimes there are things I don't understand. I don't bother trying to understand those things. I just put the text away, knowing that next time I read them I may suddenly understand them.

A JOURNEY OF A FEW CENTIMETERS

Question: How can we get out of the sense of limitedness, when we need the body and five elements to experience a wider perception?

Gurudev: The body and its five elements are as important as a car is important to get us from here to Delhi. But other than that, a car serves no purpose to us. It does not make us feel good. It does not nourish us. It does not fulfill us.

Yet we take care of the car. We make sure the tires have air. We make sure the body of the car is in good shape. We make sure there is petrol, or gas. We make sure of all these things because we realize the car is important in getting us safely from here to Delhi.

We take even better care of the car when we know we're going on a six- or eight- or ten-hour journey. If we just have to go from here to Haridwar, and it's a five-minute journey, we don't worry so much about the condition of the vehicle.

In the same way, the only importance the body—in which the Self dwells—has for the Self is to get the mind to travel from the body to the Self. And that distance is only a few centimeters.

The *Upaniṣads* ask us, "What is not attainable through the body?"

So, we understand that the body is good. We love it. We take care of it. We feed it well. Because we know it is the vehicle through which we go from the experience of being limited to the experience of the infinite.

Question: Can meditation and contemplation be categorized as austerities?

Gurudev: They are a kind of austerity, definitely. When the sage Vasiṣṭha talks about austerity, the kinds of examples he gives are standing on one foot and walking around naked. Nowadays, some people claim, "Oh, I don't eat cereal" or "I don't do this" or "I don't do that." These supposed austerities show no real attainment. Coming here to Haridwar for the past fifteen years, I have seen sādhus who are very well versed in the scriptures. But as far as any kind of what you might call social attainment in the West, that is almost zero.

One has to ask, "How much of their knowledge has been applied in their life?" Perhaps we can say the knowledge they have read has been recorded in their mind. That's about it. They are like an audio or a videotape player that records and stores all the information, but is unaffected by that information.

So what we want to do through contemplation is reach a great attainment.

THE GURU'S JOB

Question: What are we really worshipping when we worship the Guru? What is devotion to the Guru?

Gurudev: Adopting something from a different culture without understanding the whole context is not helpful. These days, people in India imitate those in the West. They don't fully understand Western ways. But they think people in the West are happy, therefore they think, "If I do all those things, such as watch television or go to discos, I'll be happy."

I tell them, "You must first understand what exists in the West. Then you'll understand the effects of those things."

In the same way, the Guru has long been an integral part of Hindu society. Basically, in India, whoever teaches is called a guru. The mother is considered the first guru. Her children learn the basics of life from her. Then the children go to school and learn from other teachers. As they grow older, they receive spiritual teachings as well as the normal, material teachings.

These days, however, we have Gurus who teach spirituality only.

As I understand things in the West, there is a breaking down of society, of family. People want a place where they can get love, where they can feel part of a family. When they go to an ashram, that sense of lack, that longing, is fulfilled. As it is fulfilled, the Guru becomes an important, integral part of their life. However, they may not use discrimination in choosing an ashram or a Guru.

Baba used to warn, "Don't have blind faith. Have faith and trust, but be aware. Look, don't just accept." He said people should be able to feel a Guru within themselves before they accept that Guru as their own.

Last weekend we celebrated the anniversary of Baba's mahāsamādhi, the day he left his physical body. I shared that I lived half my life with Baba. He was very important to me. Today, as I think of him, of course I remember the times with him, but what is most important is the feeling, the presence, he evoked within me.

If someone were to ask, "Who is Baba?" I would say he is a presence I feel within myself. Whenever I chant or speak or meditate, I feel the presence of the Guru tattva, or Guru principle. The job of any Guru is to evoke that feeling, that presence, within an individual.

Question: Do you ever have the feeling—I mean within the role you play—that you can project an energy toward someone?

Gurudev: I believe that the purpose of one who sits on the Guru's seat is to share the grace and bestow the blessings that come through that being, that person. In that moment, I think, the best thing is to allow oneself to be a vessel, to be an instrument, through which grace can pass. Instead of choosing this person or that person to receive energy, I think one allows the energy, the grace, to make its own choice.

Of course, people do come and request special prayers and blessings. Then the Guru prays on their behalf that their problem or situation be alleviated and that they feel whole or happy or whatever they want. In this respect, the Guru should pray for an individual, but otherwise one should let the energy flow and pray that everybody may receive grace and blessings.

Question: Is it possible to progress to a high degree without a Guru, without daily practice?

Gurudev: Should I leave the room?

Baba would say that whenever we wish to learn something, we seek out a good teacher. The Guru is the one who teaches you about yoga, about spirituality.

Question: Perhaps having a Guru creates dependence?

Gurudev: We see gurus who pop up from nowhere and call themselves incarnations or avatars. They present themselves to the world without actually having gone through a process of training with a master.

At the same time, people today are so hungry for knowledge and want so much to belong, that they will join just about anybody who happens to come along. They think, "This is the best thing that ever happened." A blind man is very grateful to anyone who enables him to see again.

I see this as I travel the world. Sometimes I purposely pick up a spiritual magazine to see who the latest big shot is, as far as gurus go. There are phases, or fads. Someone is at the top of the pile for a short time, and a while later a new one comes along. Then he or she peaks, and people find another one. So it goes.

But the seeker must ask, "Why?"

In a way, I blame the seeker, not the guru. Why does a guru become idolized? Because the disciples want it.

There is a little pamphlet that Krishnamurti put out. It was written in French and translated into English. It lists the ten top things you need to know if you want to be a guru. One thing it says is that if you don't know the answer to a question, you should just smile. The disciple will think he is not ready to know the answer yet. Or if you don't know the subject a disciple is discussing, you should just go into meditation. Don't delve into that subject because the disciple might know more than you, and you might end up in trouble. Whoever wrote it did so in jest, but there is a certain amount of truth to it.

So many different kinds of people lived with Baba, studied with him, hung around him. Following his passing, a bunch of them around the world said, "Baba told me to do this. He told me to be a Guru." They use techniques to control others. I don't want to go into what they do or how some twist the meaning of things he said so that it is useful for them. I figure this is the world, and all kinds of people exist within it.

Baba would say that if you buy a case of apples, there may be some rotten ones. And those rotten ones indicate to you that the others are not rotten. In the same way, he would say, the gurus who are not cooked let you know who is a true Guru. A true Guru would never make a disciple dependent on him. Whenever anybody came to Baba and asked, "What should I do? Should I do this or that?" he would always say, "Do what you think is best."

Many people want the Guru to tell them what to do. Then they are happy because they don't have to think for themselves and make tough decisions. This is true in the guru business, and in other businesses, as well.

But if the Guru doesn't tell people what they want to hear, they say, "Well, you are not for me!" And they go and find someone else who will tell them what to do.

One of the biggest questions around Baba was "Should I get married?"

He would say, "Do what you think is best."

The next day, the individual would reappear with the person he or she was in love with and ask, "Do you think it is good for my sādhanā if I marry this person?"

Baba would say, "Your sādhanā is your sādhanā. Whether you marry or not, your sādhanā will go on. So do what you think is best." He would throw the responsibility to decide back onto them.

Somebody once asked Baba, "Are you able to look into my mind, read it, and tell me what is going on?"

Baba replied, "Why would I want to know the filth going on in your mind?"

When you live in the awareness of Truth, you stay in that awareness and do not become caught in the play.

As the Sufis say, "Beware all those who would stab the egoless one, for there is nobody to stab."

Ego is there because one thinks, "I am who I am." When something nice is said, the ego is happy, elated. And when something bad is said, it is depressed, sad. But for a being who lives in the awareness "I am Consciousness," praise and blame have no effect. It is only because we associate with "I am the doer" that we get caught in all these things.

I spent my babyhood and childhood years in the ashram. That is probably the best time of life to live in an ashram. First, you are molded the right way. Second, you hear things you would never otherwise hear. People think you don't understand, so they speak their mind in front of you. In front of the Guru, a person may show love and devotion. But as soon as the Guru is gone, or the person is in a secret, private corner, he shares his real thoughts and feelings.

One of the things Baba shared just before he took me with him for the first time to tour the world was, "Remember, you will see a lot of things. Baba knows. Don't get involved in any of it."

The normal tendency is to think, "That's not how it should be. This is how it should be. That's not what Baba wants. This is what he wants." His message was "Don't get involved."

Whether you look at the ashram or the world, we are all living out our karma.

USING THE GURU AS A CRUTCH

Question: You were talking about people using other people as a crutch. Can't God also be a crutch?

Gurudev: When I say *God*, I don't mean God as somebody else or something different from me. When I talk about God, I talk about God within me.

When I spoke about using somebody as a crutch, I was referring directly to the Guru. Instead of taking responsibility for their own spiritual growth, some people use the Guru as a crutch. For example, somebody asks, "Why are you doing this?" And they say, "I don't know. My Guru told me."

Or somebody tells them, "This is not good for you. You shouldn't be doing this." And they say, "I don't know. This is what the śakti wants me to do."

Rather than saying, "This is what I feel" or "This is what I want to do," people use the Guru as a crutch.

When people asked Baba about something, one thing he liked to do was throw their question back to them. He would say, "What do you think is good?"

People would try to rephrase their question, thinking, "Maybe I'll outsmart him and he will give me an answer." But he would always ask what they thought. In this way, the person had to think for himself. He had to find out what he wanted, what he felt was right.

Of course, in this process, you might make mistakes. You might do things that are wrong. Yet you learn from that. You learn to listen to God within you, instead of just seeing God in somebody else and saying, "Oh, God is over there. That person has realized God. I haven't realized God. So let me run to him. Since he has realized God, I can ask him all my questions. All my problems will be solved, and I won't have to worry." That is what I meant by using somebody as a crutch.

When Muktānanda left his body, some people were very mad at him. They felt he had betrayed them because he hadn't given them enlightenment before he died. Now, they wondered, who was going to do it for them?

It is fine if you want to have a Guru, and you want to worship that Guru. But you have to always bear in mind that you are, and you should be, responsible for yourself. You can't place blame or say, "He will do it all for me." I think this is important, especially on the spiritual path.

THE ORIGIN OF MIND

Question: What is the origin of mind?

Gurudev: Shaivism describes the mind as Consciousness that has become limited. In Sanskrit, the mind is called *citta* and Consciousness is called *cit*. They say cit becomes citta; Consciousness becomes limited. The whole process of sādhanā is to reverse this and to take us back to being pure Consciousness.

Patañjali describes in depth how the mind functions. And Vedānta talks about the mind as four different instruments: the mind, the intellect, the subconscious mind, and the ego. The mind, or *manas*, is that with which you think, and with which you see and process all thoughts. The intellect, or *buddhi*, is that with which you decide what you will do and what you will not do. The subconscious memory, or citta, they say, is like a safe deposit in which you store everything. You may not be conscious of it happening, yet what you see, what you hear, what you are told—all of that is stored. And finally, the ego, or *ahaṁkāra*. The ego is what gives you the sense "I am this individual. I am a… whatever it is you think you are." It also gives you the pride that you get caught in.

Vedānta talks about slowly becoming free of all the parts of the mind.

As long as the mind processes everything, so many problems arise. You aren't clear: Should I? Shouldn't I? Maybe I will. Maybe I won't. However, as the mind becomes still, the intellect also starts to dissolve. Then all decisions and impulses arise from within, from the Self. They aren't processed through the mind. The subconscious also does not exist anymore, because the fire of yoga has burned it, or purified it. Whatever was stored there is gone.

Of course, the last thing to go is the ego, the individuality. But when that too is gone, then citta has become cit again. The mind has returned to Consciousness.

It's not so easy to attain, of course. We have been brought up to identify with so many things. We're told, "You are this. You are that," and so on.

There's a great story about a little boy, maybe five or six years old, who gets lost in the supermarket. He is crying. A guy comes up to him and says, "What happened?" He says, "I lost my mommy. I lost mommy." The guy says, "Okay, okay, just relax. We'll sort this out." He says, "Tell me, what's your name? We'll announce it, and your mommy will come."
The child says, "Johnny."
And the guy says, "What's your last name? Johnny what?" The child thinks and thinks and thinks. He can't recall. The guy says, "Keep thinking."
Finally, the child says, "Johnny Don't." He says, "My last name is Don't."
Why did the boy say that? Because mommy always says, "Johnny, don't do this. Johnny, don't go there. Johnny, don't…"

This is a very simple story about how we hold onto things. The subconscious mind holds all the impressions, the saṁskāras, from our experiences in this world. This is what the scriptures say drives our actions, what creates our karma. And this is what we want to become free of.

I always tell people to remember that it's a process. It's not as if somebody can tell you "sit" and your mind will instantly become still. You have to do many things in order to reach the state in which your mind is still.

However, as you watch your unfoldment back to Consciousness, and watch yourself becoming whole again, things will start falling into place. Everything you have read and heard will start to make sense.

If you look at it in pieces now, none of it makes sense. If you want all of it to blossom at once, that won't happen, either. When a flower opens, it opens slowly. Finally what's in the center is revealed. That is how it is with life, also. Slowly, gradually, you open. And then you understand your fullness, your wholeness.

Question: What techniques can you suggest to somebody to change the thought process from negative to positive?

Gurudev: That is a very simple question. Tell him to dwell on the positive! Truly speaking, that's all the scriptures say you have to do.

But then family and friends always reinforce the negative. Like Johnny Don't. They say, "You're bad." "You never eat the right things." "You don't know what to say." "You don't know how to speak."

Of course, you then go more and more toward the negative, toward self-doubt. You think, "He's always going to say I can't do it. My older brothers do it, and my younger sisters do it. This one does it, and that one does it. Just not me. God, why not me?"

The negative always seems to come forth. It's the same when you read the newspaper. Instead of first asking about positive things, a reporter asks about all the negative things. For some reason, humans love that. We love controversy. We love fights. Even though we say we don't, we love a juicy story that is filled with all this stuff.

So you have to reverse the process. You turn away from the negative thoughts. Instead, you look at the positive things, and reinforce those within yourself.

This is essentially what we are doing when we meditate, when we chant, when we repeat the mantra. All of these are ways of changing the way we think from "I am this limited person, this individual" to "I am great. I am wonderful. I am God."

In the *Bhagavad Gītā*, Lord Kṛṣṇa tells Arjuna, "This mind is like a sailboat on the open waters. The wind blows and it catches the sail, and you don't have any way to control it." Therefore, Kṛṣṇa says, "Through practice and dispassion, you will be able to bring your mind under control."

DOES GOD EXIST?

Question: This afternoon we discussed whether God exists, and in the end, the majority believed God exists. What is your perspective on that?

Gurudev: This will always be a question until one becomes established in the experience of God.

You wonder: Why do bad things happen to good people? Or why do bad things happen at all? Why is there war? If God is compassionate, loving, and kind, how can these evil, negative things happen? There is doubt.

The usual idea is that God is somebody or something with form. When you say "God," you might think of Gaṇeśa, Śiva, Pārvatī, or a Guru you worship. But you have to go beyond that and realize that God is energy, or śakti.

We don't see the electricity that flows through a wire, yet as soon as the switch is turned off, we know it was there. When no energy is flowing in the wire, the light will not work. The bulb is there. The wire is there. The fixture is there. Everything is there. But one simple action—turning the switch off—turns the light off.

In the same way, the physical body is there, everything is there, but when that energy we call God—or what Shaivism calls Consciousness—is gone, this body is inert. It no longer works. You don't have to see or feel that energy to know that when it is not there, the body is called a corpse. This very simple example allows us to believe that God exists.

We don't love each other because of our bodies or our minds. It is only because of the existence of the Self, or *Ātman*, that we can love, accept, and believe in each other. Therefore, discover what that Self is.

The *Upaniṣads* say, "The Self—or God—is not what is thought of by the mind, but by which the mind thinks."

We want to understand God. Yet, we can't because God is so vast, and our mind is so small, so limited. Therefore, we also must become vast. We must expand ourselves. We must become great. The shift has to take place within. And when that shift takes place, the experience is also there.

The sun rises and sets every day. The seasons change. Today is the first day of autumn. If you watch the seasons and everything else happening in the universe, you wonder who is running things. Who's doing all of this? It's surely not humans. No computer expert is programming the sun to set and rise or the moon to rise and set. No program is making it autumn now and later winter. There is no way humans could do that. We'd create chaos! As advanced as we think we are, we aren't really that advanced.

Baba used to say there was no reason to seek God because God already exists within us. All we need do is become aware of His existence.

I wouldn't say Baba convinced me of the existence of God. But the experience of being with him and doing what he taught us convinced me. When that direct experience is there, it can't be taken away or shaken by anybody.

We can discuss the existence of God. We can talk and argue about it. This has been done for ages. But it's only when we sit with ourselves and experience it that we realize God exists. He exists in the form of energy, which runs everything.

Science has advanced a lot in modern times, yet scientists have not captured that which makes everything work. If we were to ask scientists to create another planet like Earth, they couldn't do it. They might try to create life on Mars. But even if they're able to do that, it won't be original life; it will just be a copy.

I believe the only way to answer this question is to understand it yourself. First, you listen to the different arguments. Then you contemplate it and think about all the viewpoints. Each person's view is true in its own way because it expresses his or her understanding. Your own view might be narrower or wider, depending on your state.

Ultimately, it is the lecture given in silence by the Guru that dissolves all doubts.

How can a lecture be given in silence? Isn't that a paradox?

After all, a lecture is given by speaking. So if the Guru sits silently and doesn't say anything, how is something being said? However, if the Guru sits silently and the disciple sits silently, then a lecture is taking place at a different level.

It is a transmission. The Guru is in touch with the Self, and in this way he leads the disciple to get in touch with the Self, as well. In silence, they communicate. The disciple may not understand that communication is taking place because he's waiting, waiting, waiting for the Guru to speak. And the Guru is waiting, waiting, waiting for the disciple to listen to himself.

I remember when Baba's ashram was small. We were young and had our different relationships with him. My relationship with him was mostly quiet. We didn't much talk, other than about sevā. I guess I was scared of him, so I stayed away. Other people thought, "Baba's my friend, my buddy." So they hung out with him and talked.

There was one American lady who was the quiet type. She used to stand at the back. One day, she thought to herself, "Baba talks to all these other people, and I stand here alone. I've come all the way from America, and he says nothing to me. He must not love me. He doesn't know who I am. He doesn't care." She was thinking all that and feeling sad. But she stayed quiet.

Then Baba called her up and asked, "Why are you crying? Do you think I don't want to talk with you, that I prefer to talk to all these people?" He paused, and then he said, "I always talk to you. Just listen. Listen to me on the inside."

She went back and she realized, "It's so true."

ĀRATĪ

Question: I don't know if I missed it, but what is the meaning behind āratī?

Gurudev: No, you didn't miss it. I didn't explain it.

In the olden days, when there was no electricity, the statue of the deity was in the center of the temple. It was very dark there. When devotees came to have darśan, the only way they could see the deity was through āratī, through the waving of a light. Even today most orthodox temples have no electric light.

When the orthodox Brahmin priests do āratī, they wave the lights to every part of the deity: face, arms, legs. They wave the lamp all the way down, then raise it back up. Then they bring it to you because in very orthodox temples, you cannot go close to the statue of the deity. Only Brahmins are allowed there. So the only way to come close to the deity you worship is through contact with the lamp that has been close to it.

Spiritually, the lamp represents the light of Consciousness that dwells within us. By waving the light to the deity or Guru we worship, we show that light of Consciousness to him. Then we internalize it by waving our hands over the light and touching our eyes or face. That's the essence of āratī.

Often an explanation is very simple. But we complicate things. So just allow yourself to experience it. It is what it is.

POWER OF MANTRA

Question: What do you mean by the mantra being powerful?

Gurudev: I mean the experience within you is powerful.

I can describe my own first mantra experience when I was fifteen. I had been with Baba since I was little because my parents went to see him all the time. On this particular day, I went with Baba to an Intensive where he was going to give initiation. I thought to myself, "How can what Baba does today be any different from what he has done for the last fifteen years in my life? I've been touched by him. I've been beaten by him. I've been spoken to by him." So I thought, "Well, nothing will happen."

But when Baba gave the mantra, and then came around and touched me, there was a power that drew me deep inside. I was only fifteen, so I had no idea what to expect. In fact, I thought nothing would happen. But I was suddenly within myself in a quiet, peaceful place. I was still aware of the outside, but no matter how much I tried to open my eyes to look around and see what was going on, I could not. I remained in that experience for almost an hour.

That is the power of mantra. It is also the faith the Guru has in the mantra, and the faith I have in the Guru. When I received the mantra, a part of me was willing to receive it.

For example, we can use the analogy that grace is like rain. It may always be falling, but if you stand under it with an open umbrella, you will say, "But I'm not getting wet." To feel the rain, to get wet, you must close the umbrella.

In us, the umbrella is the mind. The mind is sitting there, waiting to be the judge. "Is it going to work? Is it not going to work? Is it real? Is it not real?"

The only way to experience the Truth is to allow the mind to stop.

The Truth is not something that can be understood with the mind. There are many things I know that I cannot explain. All I can do is share in the best possible way, and hope I can convey the feeling. The feeling is what is important.

This is why we have satsaṅg. When we come together, we create that feeling. Each person goes to the same inner space and touches it.

When you are in that open space and receive the mantra from someone who fully believes in it—and who has done it not just a few times, but for a long time—you can have a powerful experience.

Sometimes people say, "I've never had that experience again."

I say, "It is a very powerful experience. If you keep pouring two hundred watts through a one hundred watt bulb, it will burn out. A moment is okay."

So the Guru ignites the desire for that feeling inside us. We feel, "I want that peace, that joy." Then the Guru says, "Okay, you can have it. But you must do these practices and get yourself there."

It's a matter of purifying the mind, purifying the ego, cleansing yourself so you can hold that state. The only reason you lose touch with it is that the mind and ego come into play. So japa and the other practices prepare you so that when the experience happens again, you can hold it.

THE VALUE OF HUMAN BIRTH

Question: Baba used to say there is no higher form than a human being. But it appears to me that the world is going downhill. I'm having a crisis of belief in the goodness of human beings. What do you have to say about that?

Gurudev: The scriptures state that a human has the ability to know his or her own Self. No other living creature in this creation of God has the ability to know its own true nature.

Each of us who is sitting in this room, in satsaṅg, has the ability to ask ourselves, "Who am I?"

However, I agree, animals sometimes appear more evolved than humans. I like to use the example of a dog. No matter how you have treated a dog, it comes lovingly to greet you when it hears you. A dog recognizes the sound of the engine of your car when it is still a block away. It recognizes the sound of your footsteps even when it still cannot see you. We as humans don't even know when we hear the doorbell ring who is at the door.

I think this situation is because we have cut ourselves off from our own inner nature.

Over thirty years of doing this work, I have come to realize that goodness exists in each and every one of us. There is no human being who does not have goodness in him or her. But circumstances and situations make people mean or cruel. Thus, if we consider ourselves to be good, we have to constantly make the effort to do good.

I think of the few hundred people who lived with Baba and the few thousand who came to see him in the various places he went. He was just one person—and he didn't speak English, he only spoke Hindi—yet he was able to have the effect he had on so many people all over the world. So if we make the effort, think of what each one of us can do in our workplace, in our family, among our friends.

Of course, not everybody enjoys satsaṅg. But satsaṅg can be done in many ways. Often we get caught in thinking satsaṅg has to be like this. We have to have a harmonium and a drum, and pictures, and tapes of chanting. No, I believe you can have satsaṅg without all the trappings. Nor is it necessary to tell people, "I'm inviting you to satsaṅg."

Think of the qualities of satsaṅg: a clean space, a space filled with beautiful flowers, that is filled with beautiful lights, a space that is fragrant, delicious food. The mantra can be played on instruments as music. If twenty-five or fifty people come to your place for July 4th or Thanksgiving or your birthday, it can be satsaṅg simply through the quality of the gathering you have.

First pick a theme you wish to share. It could be a theme from Baba's teachings, for example. Then find a friend, perhaps someone you know from satsaṅg, to conspire with you. Together, figure out how you will present this theme at your gathering. Because people will ask, "Where did you learn this?"

Basically satsaṅg means good company. I think that is what society lacks today. You go to a bar, and it is crowded, with no space to sit. People have to shout to hear each other. They get drunk—thinking that's how they will get relaxed and happy, only to find out the next morning that they didn't do anything except disappear for a few hours.

At the ashram, we asked the question "How do we change the conversation?" We talk about what we can do so we are able to see the world from a different perspective, so we don't get too caught up in worldly life.

Often when I am in the United States, I buy *Time* and *Newsweek* regularly and read them. But this time I said, "I don't want to do that." And I didn't. Fortunately nobody gave them to me, either. When you read all that, you go, "Oh my God, it's a horrible world. It's a cruel place for cruel people."

As we travel, we meet people who are wonderful. I have found in the ashram and in the homes I visit, the food is prepared fresh, and everybody loves to eat it. We learned from Baba that this is one of the ways through which you feed people love.

If you go to most homes nowadays, people buy frozen food at the store. When they get home, they throw it in the microwave. They don't even put it in a dish. And they use plastic spoons.

That way, they don't have to wash anything. They don't even have to wash their hands.

You ask yourself, "What have we done to life?" We have frozen life. We zap it when we want it. When we decide we want to be loving or happy or friendly or nice, we have to thaw ourselves out. Otherwise we remain frozen as we go through society.

California is a little bit different, I would say. But in most places, most people have what I call sour looks. They don't smile. They don't look you in the eye. They don't talk to you. So many fears exist.

When you see this, you ask, "What can I do?"

I suggest we begin with our family and friends. If you are a teacher, you can invite your students and their parents. Find ways to incorporate the spiritual teachings through a theme, as I was saying.

I was reading about art teachers and therapists. They observe how a child draws, and figure out from that what is going on within the child. A happy, loving picture means the child is happy and well adjusted. An angry or disturbed picture might suggest the child is asking for help.

If you read Baba's books, especially his questions and answers, you will find he often quoted the scriptures: "It is not easy to obtain a human birth, so take care of it and use it wisely."

The scriptures also say that having obtained a human birth, if you don't put it to good use, you are no different from an animal. You are in the body of a human, but if you behave like an animal, you are not human.

People who perform the kinds of acts to which you referred have not realized the human quality in themselves. They are being animals, we could say. And they are in the company of other animal-like people, so that is the quality that is fostered in them. They may belong to a gang or other kinds of groups to which such people belong.

One day, however, it dawns on them that they could become a good person.

However, they don't know where to go to become a good person. In modern-day society, if a person thinks, "I want to hang out somewhere different," it's not easy to know where to go. When I grew up, we could go to any home or any other parent and say, "I'm mad at my parents, I don't want to go home." That parent would say, "Okay, spend the evening here." I think we should create homes or places now that have an openness about them, where such people could go.

In Baba's time, there were about thirty small ashrams where people could go every day. I don't know what the schedule was because I was not there. I think one day there was chanting. One day there was a video. One day there was a text, such as the Śiva Mahiṁnaḥ Stotram. One day was a designated satsang day, when you could bring a new friend. One day was probably sevā. Every day something happened. You could go there and participate.

The three hundred plus centers Baba started were also what we could call safe havens. You could go once a week and chant and meditate. In those two hours, you could rejuvenate yourself for the week.

Temples, churches, ashrams—all these religious, spiritual, holy places are there so that when a human forgets his humanness and becomes animal-like, he can go to such a place.

In the twelve years from 1970 to 1982, we saw the amount of effort Baba put forth to share his teachings, to share his wisdom, to share himself, really. It can't go to waste. He himself believed in all that he talked about. He had no doubt in that which he shared with us.

So we have to do what we can. We make sure we do good things, that we don't become mean. This has been the challenge for many who stayed on the path. We simply do our practices. We follow the teachings. We constantly evolve ourselves so we become better humans, rather than animals.

Whatever you received from Baba in the years you spent with him, I think you have to keep it strong. And then find different ways to share it in whatever you do in the world.

Question: In Santa Monica, I had an amazing experience. But since Baba left, as much as I try, I can't get it back. The path seems much harder. There's something about being enfolded in that embryonic space that feeds you on a daily level, that you don't get when you're living on your own. I haven't chanted in a long time, so this satsaṅg has been very nourishing for me.

Gurudev: I think that's why Baba created centers around the world. His idea was that people would gather in living rooms like this, and feed each other.

I talk about two kinds of practices. One is an individual practice, and one is a collective practice. An individual practice is something you do on your own every day, to become established in the teachings, in your understanding. Collective practice is what we do maybe once a week. Or if you live in an ashram, then every day.

I've never lived outside an ashram, except for a few months in 1986. Even then, I lived with my parents, so practice was easy. But I can understand what you are saying.

That's why I like reading the ashram magazine with stories from the early days. It takes me there, to that feeling, to that experience. I think what each of us has to do in our own space is create that embryonic feeling you mentioned.

When we first started Shanti Mandir, we had a one-hour satsaṅg on Wednesday evenings. People would come after work. We did the āratī. We did a text chant. And then we meditated. There were no meals, no talking. One woman always brought a packet of Andes mints. At the end of satsaṅg, she stood at the door with a tray of mints. Everybody took one—some took two—and then they went home. Although only a few of us gathered every Wednesday, the feeling we had was always wonderful.

I think wherever you live, you can make an effort to create satsaṅg. It doesn't matter if you only have a few people.

One woman here has started a satsaṅg wherever she goes. Her husband doesn't participate, but I always tell her, "He lets you do it. That's his offering." He loves his horses; that's his meditation. He loves his work; that's his meditation. For Mother's Day, he came to satsaṅg as an offering to her because he knew that's where she wanted to be.

Sometimes we get caught up in our ideas about how things should be. For this reason, I talk about acceptance and patience. I relate to what you are saying because when we are on the road, we look forward to being back in the ashram. We know the schedule there. We know the feeling we get. Yet, when we travel, we try to carry that same feeling with us. I think, in your own way, you have to find the various elements that will create a feeling like that.

Of course, it is extraordinary when a large number of people come together and chant. I often say that the point of going to any religious gathering is not to see what is happening, but to feel the devotion.

For example, in India, this January and February, we have the Kumbh Melā. A few million people will be there. Some people won't go because they are scared of being crushed or getting lost. But I believe one goes to feel the excitement of all that devotion.

THE SIMPLICITY OF DEVOTION

Question: During the Kumbh Melā, tens of thousands came to Haridwar to fill containers with Ganges water. What is the act of faith they were performing, and how can we as Westerners learn from that?

Gurudev: I think to see the simplicity of their devotion is the greatest lesson all of us can take, whether we are Indians or Westerners.

These simple folk, who live in small huts, in villages, come hundreds of kilometers by bus—or sometimes even walk—and then go that same distance back, just to take the Ganges water to their home or their temple. They bathe their deity with that water. That is the purpose of their carrying the water at the time of Śivarātri, the festival of Śiva.

When you study the scriptures and read the stories of holy men who have experienced divinity, you see that what has given them the experience is their pure, simple devotion.

Question: Can you put into words what faith, or devotion, is?

Gurudev: In the material world, the simplest example is when a man meets a woman, or a woman meets a man, and they feel a connection. They are drawn to each other. There is a feeling, which we call love, that arises in the heart. Now, to explain what happens is not so simple. Yet we know the feeling is there.

When a spiritual or religious person sees a deity or a Guru or a holy man, the same feeling arises in his heart. Whereas in a human relationship, we want something from the other person, in a spiritual relationship, we don't desire anything other than to have that feeling continuously.

Simply put, devotion is that feeling arising within your heart. It may be just a little taste, a little glimpse, of what can arise if you allow yourself to be in the state of pure devotion at all times.

When the scriptures say be like a little child, they mean to have this innocence. A child does not think, "If I do this, this will happen or that will happen." He simply is who he is. When we have this same simplicity, then devotion wells up within us. The village folk you mentioned at the Kumbh Melā are, in a way, like children. Though they are adults, they're not encumbered by all the material thoughts most people have in the world today. They simply believe, "I will carry this water from the Ganges to my temple, and I will be sanctified. I will be liberated." They don't wonder, "When will I be liberated?" or "How will I be liberated?" They just know "I will be."

Simply having that thought is important. Of course, you know it may not happen now, in this moment. But somehow, sometime, it will happen. God willing.

Question: Many people come to the Kumbh Melā to receive the blessings of great sages who rarely appear in public. How does a person receive the blessings? What actually happens?

Gurudev: The analogy that comes to mind is that if it's raining and you go outside, you will get wet. But if you take an umbrella, you will be protected from the rain.

So if a person goes to a sage with an open mind, an open heart, his vessel will be open to receive the blessings that are being poured on him, that are being given.

Whether you go as a seeker or a visitor or a tourist, I recommend having an open heart and mind. Try not to be judgmental or rationalize what you see. Just say, "Okay, this is happening." Witness it and allow yourself to digest what you have seen.

In my thirty years of growing up around Baba and of living in ashrams, many things took place that one might not understand in the moment, that seemed odd or strange or out of place or irrational. But as time went on, it would dawn on one that the incident or experience was bearing this fruit. It was possible to say, "This is what is actually happening."

I can't say that I was with Baba because I thought I wanted his grace, his blessings. My parents took me to the ashram, so I went. And I just loved being around Baba's energy. I was drawn to it because it felt good. But now as I look back at the years I spent with him and at what I received from him, I see its effect. It led me to do certain practices, and those are bearing fruit.

If you throw a seed out in nature, it becomes a tree. If you nurture it, it grows a little bit faster. If you don't do anything, it takes a little time, but it grows anyway.

In the same way, if a seeker comes and feels, "I really want this," he will receive what he wants. If he comes just with an open mind and heart, he will still receive it. It may take more time, but it will bear fruit.

The purpose of a holy man, a saint, is to give blessings. The sun shines upon everybody, without distinguishing between high and low. A tree gives shade, whether the person is a weary traveler or plans to cut down that tree after he has rested in its shade. In the same way, a sage gives his blessings to anybody who comes into his presence. Each person receives the blessings according to his capacity and his understanding.

SANĀTAN DHARMA

Question: As a Mahāmandaleshwar, part of your responsibility is to uphold the sanātan dharma. What exactly is the sanātan dharma?

Gurudev: The *sanātan* dharma is known today as the Hindu religion or the Hindu philosophy. Before the word *Hindu* was coined, the philosophy we followed was know as sanātan dharma, or simply dharma.

Dharma means the law that sustains life. Sanātan means eternal.

We believe the Hindu philosophy, or Vedic philosophy, has existed for many thousands of years and was not created by any particular individual. It has been followed by many people around the world for a long time. So our duty as Mahāmandaleshwars and Gurus is to make sure the teachings of the *Vedas* continue; that people become aware that they must live good, righteous, honest, straightforward lives, and that whatever actions they perform will have consequences.

It might seem hard to live in today's world according to what is taught in the *Vedas*. Yet I think if you try to follow that, you can have a happy, peaceful life. Simply understanding the philosophy of karma gives an understanding of the diversities in this world. You see how everything that happens is the outcome of actions that have been performed by all of us, and that all those actions are intertwined in some way.

Question: Is it possible to boil sanātan dharma down to a simple set of guidelines or is it a complex set of laws?

Gurudev: The actual philosophy is very simple. However, when different people teach it, they give it their own flavor, and it seems to get complicated. You have the essential philosophy, and then you have all the commentaries given by different people.

The Vedic philosophy is written in Sanskrit. So unless you know Sanskrit, you have to read the translations in Hindi or

English or whatever your language is. Then you have to accept whatever the translator has given as the meaning.

Now people are trying to revive Sanskrit so more people can speak it, read it, and understand it. If that can happen, then the philosophy of sanātan dharma can be understood more simply.

Question: Is it possible for you to talk about the nature of the universal law?

Gurudev: Simply put, sanātan dharma wants us to live a wholesome life. The world over, people are trying to be organic these days—for their bodies, for the Earth, for air, for water. Sanātan dharma also teaches us to be holistic, to be organic. Of course, it does so without using those terms.

Sanātan dharma teaches us to be kind to nature, to be kind to animals, to be loving to other human beings. In this way, it is teaching us to take care of each other, to realize that one needs the other to live.

The *Upaniṣads* teach us to speak the truth, not just in our work, but in our actions.

Some people think, "If I always tell the truth, that's enough." But it is said that you should live your life in Truth in such a way that whatever you say becomes truth. In fact, we have stories in the scriptures of sages in the olden days who would say something and it would happen.

The guidelines have been laid out, so try to follow them. Go along that path as much as you can.

Question: On your right is a picture of Ādi Śaṅkarācārya. Who is he and why is he so respected?

Gurudev: Ādi Śaṅkarācārya is considered to be the incarnation of Lord Śiva himself; therefore, he has the name Śaṅkara. Śaṅkara is one of the names of Śiva. Ācārya means teacher.

When he saw that Buddhism was flourishing and the philosophy of sanātan dharma was slowly being hidden away, Śiva felt, "I must reincarnate and make sure the philosophy of the *Vedas* continues to flourish." So he came in the incarnation of Ādi Śaṅkara, who was born in South India.

At a very young age, he left home and revived the tradition of the sādhus and swamis. He organized the monks into proper orders, which became know as the Daśanāmi *sampradāya*. Daśanāmi means the ten names.

Anyone who becomes a swami today is grateful to Ādi Śaṅkara for continuing the sanātan dharma. Ashrams that belong to one of the ten orders he created have his picture. Or they may have his statue.

In the corner of our ashram in Kankhal, India, we have a roundabout known as Śaṅkarācārya Chowk, where his statue is installed. On April 30, which is his birthday, or Śaṅkarācārya *jayanti*, people gather there and form a procession. People from different ashrams come out to welcome the procession, and talks are given about his philosophy and what he did.

Everything he did was done in a very short time because he left his body at the age of thirty-two. He revived the philosophy of the *Vedas*. And then he went into the Himalayas and just disappeared.

TO GET TO THE FORMLESS, START WITH THE FORM

Question: What is the purpose and role of ritual in spiritual development?

Gurudev: We believe the mind needs a form to focus upon.
Suppose somebody tells you, "Just love your Self."
Then the question arises: "What is the Self?" You can't see the Self. So you may not understand what that means.

But if a form is given to the Self—whether it is Śiva or Rāma or Kṛṣṇa or one of the myriad other deities—then it becomes easier. You know "this is the deity I'm drawn to, whom I have affection for, whom I love."

In the *Bhagavad Gītā*, Arjuna asks Kṛṣṇa, "Which is the better path: to worship the form or to worship the formless?"

Kṛṣṇa says, "To get to the formless, you must start with the form."

A devotee starts by worshiping and honoring the idol or statue of the deity. He performs ceremonies to that being. At the end of the ritual, meditation occurs. As time goes on, the difference between the devotee and the deity, his beloved, starts to disappear.

Of course, priests and other people who perform rituals may only meditate for one or two minutes after they finish the verses. But the idea is to actually meditate upon the deity. As you meditate, you imbibe the qualities of that being or of that Guru. You invoke those same qualities within yourself.

We also have what is called *manasa* pūjā, or mental worship. You sit and meditate, and the whole ritual happens on the inside. Slowly you internalize the process and become free from the external worship.

WHAT IS ENLIGHTENMENT?

Question: What is Truth?

Gurudev: Truth is the experience we have when we are happy and content, and when nothing needs to be said. We feel full. We don't want anything from anyone. We are just here.

Question: What is the end point you are talking about? Is there a permanent state of altered consciousness that we're working toward?

Gurudev: I think that seeking the experience of enlightenment is valid. If you read Bhagavān Nityānanda's book, you see that he talks about liberation again and again and again. In fact, all Indian scriptures talk about liberation, or enlightenment.

The question is what is enlightenment?

I love to quote Jñāneśvar Mahārāj, who said that enlightenment means enlightenment from the idea of enlightenment.

We tend to have a concept of what liberation is. But when you really contemplate it, you realize it's just freedom. For example, when you allow yourself to let go into a chant, there is simply ecstasy. There are no thoughts, no worries, no problems. You're swaying, clapping, singing, lost in the chant. And when it stops, you're still in that state.

These are glimpses of enlightenment, of liberation. Of course, the mind comes back and says, "Okay, now let's go and do whatever needs to be done."

I'm sure you've heard different people share their experience of śaktipāt, of their initial awakening. Often it's like a teaser one gets at the beginning of sādhanā. You think, "That's what I want!" You know that is your goal. And then you work toward it.

As people seek and continue on with their practices, sometimes they start to wonder, "Well, that initial taste was nice, but does it really exist?"

It does exist. But how much fuel you put into the process of letting go and how much you take care of and nurture that experience are in your hands.

Baba is a great example. What did he do? He left home and spent almost twenty-five years traveling, studying, seeking. Finally, after all those years of frustration, he reconnected with his Guru, Bhagavān Nityānanda. He received initiation and then spent another nine years doing nothing but waking up in the morning... meditating for four to five hours... reading for a couple of hours... sleeping... getting up... having a little bite to eat... meditating... going back to sleep... getting up... reading... having a little bit of satsaṅg—or sometimes no satsaṅg... meditating, and then going back to sleep around eleven o'clock.

We have to ask ourselves if we have the capacity, the strength, to do that without feeling bored or frustrated or getting caught up in all the different emotions that arise.

In *Play of Consciousness*, Baba mostly talks about all the great things that happened. Yet we know that in the midst of his ecstatic experiences, there had to be other things he didn't write about. I think the sages leave out these kinds of things that we already know. They want to tell us about what we don't know. But then, because Baba didn't tell us about that which we know, we think maybe he was different. We think he didn't really know what we are going through.

Yoga is a process. It allows you to let go a little bit more each time, to stretch a bit more. And that little bit more stretches until you come to a point where your concepts and attachments and limitations drop away. They're gone. But if you don't engage in this process, that point will never come.

If you look at your state now, I think you'll see a shift has taken place over the years. Your understanding has continued to grow and deepen. Your mind is calmer than it was twenty years ago. Your acceptance of situations is greater. Before you act, you stop for a moment and ask, "Why am I doing this? What is the purpose?" To me, all these are leading toward the goal of liberation, of enlightenment.

EMOTION IS ENERGY

Question: When it comes to emotions welling up, is your suggestion to experience the emotion or just remain detached and see it as another form of māyā?

Gurudev: It depends on the individual. Some love to delve into their emotions. Some love to see them as māyā.

Emotion is just energy, and how you use that energy is in your hands.

If you allow the mind to go into an emotion, you sink, sink, sink. Then you have to do something to come out of it.

As an emotion is arising, you can repeat a mantra that you like or you can chant. That way, you don't go into the emotion. At the same time, you're dealing with it because you're letting it out. When you've finished chanting, you are in a happier, more ecstatic state, and the release of the emotion has also happened.

Question: Sometimes I find myself one step away from acting out an emotion, but I don't. Still, it does take a toll on me.

Gurudev: To release emotion, you can perform an action that takes a lot of physical energy, such as scrubbing the bathroom. We always did this in the ashram. You take a toothbrush and start cleaning. By the time you are finished, you're exhausted and ready to go to sleep.

Baba would go walking. It was his way of releasing energy. Of course, walking is good for the body, but it is also a release. You just walk. There's no responsibility, no need to think about anything.

I go for a drive and chant. When one deals with people a lot, one picks up different energies. A drive for me is just ten minutes, to collect some mail or go to the health food store. When I drive, I drive alone. No one is talking to me, saying, "We need to do this and that. We need to go here and there." I am just driving—a little faster, a little slower—and about twenty minutes later I'm back.

There are always jobs to be done. In that moment when you're about to act out of emotion, you say, "Okay, I'm going to do that job I've been avoiding for a long time."

When you get involved in an activity—whether it is gardening or whatever you don't like to do—your mind gets totally absorbed. If you are frustrated or angry, you will probably do that same job in much less time than usual because you are full of energy that needs to be released.

Definitely, a release needs to take place. Holding emotions in does not achieve anything. It's like shaking a soda bottle: you must open it, otherwise the top may pop.

Quite a few of the sicknesses we face in the world today are created through frustration, anger, stress—all the emotions people bottle up inside and don't release.

BE LIKE A FLUTE

Question: I went through a very intense period a while ago and I found myself giving advice. When I witnessed it, it didn't feel like me saying the words. Did I tap into my higher Self? Could you shed any light on that?

Gurudev: I think all of us have wisdom within. Just as Consciousness is there, wisdom also is there. But when we identify with our limitations, we don't identify with the wisdom, the greatness, that dwells within us.

When we allow ourselves to be big—and in that bigness not have attachment to what others will think or what they will say or feel—we can actually give wisdom. And we also are astounded.

People often ask me, "Where did you read all this? Where did you learn all this?"

I say, "Well, I lived with Baba. I'm sure that during all those years of sitting with him some knowledge got in."

The sages tell us to be like a flute. If we become hollow, the śakti, the grace, can flow through us. So each of us can try to be like a reed through which Consciousness flows.

When that happens, you can be amazed at the sounds that come through you. But you have to remember at the same time that it is not you but the greater Consciousness that's creating that sound.

For this reason, it is one thing to know "I am Consciousness," but it is something else to actually live in that awareness at all times. It takes being in a great state.

You love coming on Mondays to chant the *Śiva Mahimnaḥ*. Like that, by finding a practice you love, you are able to connect to that divinity, that wisdom, which is unlimited within. When you do that, it's like opening a little window within yourself. Each time you do the practice, you open the window a little bit more.

Wisdom is always there. It's just that people don't tap into it because they are afraid or distracted. If you step back from being limited, you can share that great wisdom with others. Just remember that it is flowing through you, that it's not something you own.

CLARITY OF MIND

Question: How does one acquire clarity of mind? What are the ways in which one can increase the clarity with which thoughts come?

Gurudev: Take the example of a room. If you have a lot of stuff in the room, you know that what you're looking for is in there somewhere. But where? You don't know because there's so much other stuff.

In the same way, when the mind has many thoughts, you know a particular thought is in there somewhere. But where?

When I walk into some rooms—like this one—it's wonderful. I can walk around without bumping into anything. On the other hand, some homes I go to have so much stuff you practically have to negotiate a pathway between all the items. You are bound to bump your foot or knee on something.

Minds are like that.

Of course, a house may be filled with clutter, but to the owner everything is valuable. He feels an emotional connection with each item. It's the same way with thoughts. People have attachments to all their thoughts. They have emotions tied to those thoughts.

People who have lots of stuff wonder, "If I had to get rid of something, what would I get rid of?" They can't decide.

In the same way, you might think, "Okay, I'm going to have fewer thoughts." But then you wonder, "What thoughts would I let go of?"

Some people can see something and remember every single detail of what they have seen. When you have a conversation with them, they want you to hear every detail, from the beginning to the end. They are only talking about one thing, but everything they have seen or done in their lifetime comes with it.

You say, "Just tell me what you really want to say."

"No, no." They expect you to hold all the details.

I think a seeker needs to create space within. At some point, you become aware that you don't want to carry with you that which is not necessary, that which is not going to serve a purpose in your life.

Creating space in this way brings clarity. Then whatever thought you are looking for is not just somewhere, it's right there.

I'm sure each individual has his own way of bringing clarity. But in general, the fewer thoughts you have, the clearer you will be.

Question: Some people might not have many thoughts, but they don't have much awareness, either.

Gurudev: I wouldn't say that people who are unaware, who are *jaḍ*, don't have many thoughts. I think they have slower rather than faster thoughts. There is nothing within them impelling them forward to do something. Therefore, they become lazy.

When Baba used the word jaḍ, he implied a heaviness, and a lack of interest. In fact, when you talk to people who are jaḍ, they often have a lot to say. But they don't have much clarity. Therefore, they don't know what they want to do. They can't decide.

In the *Bhagavad Gītā*, Kṛṣṇa says to Arjuna that nothing he is about to do is new.

Swami Chinmayānanda comments on this, saying that a person might think, "If I'm not beginning anything new, then why begin anything?"

Everything has been happening over time. Though it may seem new to the individual who's creating it, something like it has been done before. So Kṛṣṇa wants Arjuna to realize, "I'm simply continuing that which has been done."

The *Upaniṣads* remind us, "Don't be lazy." That means that sometimes you must force yourself to do things. If you have clarity as well as the desire to do something, I think you will do it.

I think more people are jaḍ and unaware than are aware. For some reason, when some people come to the path of spirituality, they become lazy. They think yoga is telling them to do nothing. But the philosophy of yoga doesn't tell you to physically stop doing anything. It tells you to quiet and still the mind, but still perform your activities in the world.

When you really understand yoga, it makes you sharp, not jaḍ. Sometimes people say, "I love Kashmir Shaivism. It's simple: everything is Consciousness."

It's not really that simple. Yes, everything is Consciousness, but you have to arrive at that understanding. It is problematic if you try to practice "Everything is Śiva" when you have not yet cast the mug—the cup—away.

The path of Vedānta takes you step by step. Although emptying your cup into the ocean may seem to happen in one instant, you have to go through the whole process. You have to get to the beach. You have to walk up to the ocean. You must have taken the cup with you. And then you have to turn the cup upside down.

Sometimes people assume that the cup, as it is, is Consciousness. In their limited state, they announce, "I am Self-realized."

You want to ask, "How can you claim you are Self-realized?"

A great sage, such as Bhagavān or Baba, lives in the experience of the Self all the time. There is never the thought, "I am now *not* realized."

A man who comes to the ashram jokes that on Mondays, Wednesdays, and Fridays he's realized. On Tuesdays, Thursdays, Saturdays, and Sundays, he's his limited self. He says, "Call me on the days I'm realized and I'll answer your question. On the other days, I'm normal, so I can have fun." Of course, he's playing with us, and he's aware that he's just playing. But some people seriously believe they are realized when they wish or choose to be.

I'd be tempted to take everything away from such people that is supposedly theirs—whether it is a home, a car, or money—and say, "I want this!"

If they are really living in that experience, they should say, "Okay, here. I'll sign it over to you."

Of course, Self-realization is just a concept in their mind. They have studied Shaivism and come to the conclusion, "I've had glimpses of the Self, so I understand what the Self is." The philosophy of Kashmir Shaivism says that the fourth state of *turīya* must flow into all the other states. Your waking, dream, and deep sleep states must have the same experience of oneness, of Consciousness, at all times.

Shaivism is like a guidebook that shows you where you can end up. Especially in the world today, I think Shaivism needs to be taught with a grain of salt, so to speak. The student has to realize that this philosophy will grant the experience. You will get there. But you cannot overnight claim, "I am there." You can't say you are there simply because you have read, "There is nothing which is not Śiva."

I've seen this in different places in the world. Of course, you can't say anything because people will think you're jealous of the fact that they are experiencing everything as Śiva. So it is best in that moment to be jaḍ and say, "I'm so sad I'm not where you are."

I hope you understand this. It's a subtle difference, but it's a big difference.

Question: I'm pondering the relationship between one's use of śakti and the ability to quiet one's mind.

Gurudev: Śakti is generated through practice.

In the olden days, one had a dynamo on a bicycle wheel and it generated light as the wheel turned. In the same way, through practice—whether it is japa or chanting the *Guru Gītā* or coming to satsaṅg—we generate śakti. And that śakti then allows us to be still and quiet.

You could say the two go hand in hand. The śakti is there, but we also have to put forth the effort to maintain quiet.

The other night, somebody said, "You know satsaṅg is good because everybody is excited, everybody is talking."

I said, "You could also know satsaṅg is good because at the

end, before they start to talk, there is a moment of stillness, of quiet."

Some people who come to satsaṅg tell me they want to go home quietly, but everybody is talking.

I say, "Who is telling you to talk? You don't have to stay for the tea and the cookie, and talk. If you're feeling good, take that feeling, say goodnight, and go home."

Yet the natural human instinct is to feel, "I'm excited now!" Then the śakti is blown. The person goes home and thinks, "I felt so good after the satsaṅg, but then I had the chai and the cookie…"

BECOME WAVES IN THE OCEAN

Question: Sometimes I feel the bliss is so overwhelming that I have to shut it down or run away. I want to know how to deal with it so I don't need to push it down or dampen it.

Gurudev: Here is a physical exercise you can try. Every day, take a pitcher or a mug of water and go down to the stream. Throw the water into the stream, and watch what happens.

The water merges into the stream. Nothing actually happens to it. Except you can't take that water back out.

What stops any of us from merging into the ocean of bliss?

Truly speaking, this is a fear everybody has. You know it and are expressing it. But if you go around the room, I'm sure everybody will say they have the same fear. Because the question arises: if I merge into the ocean of bliss, what will happen to the "little me"?

What happens to the little me is like what happens when you take that pitcher and throw the water into the stream. There is no more "me," no more "I." There is no more "my" pitcher of water either. It all becomes one with the water.

So we try to go to that place within where there is no "I" vibrating as a separate individual.

For example, when you chant, and are able to let go, you become immersed in that place for at least a few moments. When this happens, the chanting is very good.

Tonight we'll chant *Hare Rāma, Hare Kṛṣṇa*, and I hope the chant takes us to that place. As the drummer, this is what I try for. But I have fifty to seventy-five other elements to work with, so I'm not always successful. If those elements come together, we get to the place where all the separate "I's" dissolve. Of course they still exist, but subjectively speaking they disappear. They become waves in that one ocean.

When we are chanting—whether it is the *Guru Gītā* or *Hare Rāma*—we don't always get to that place. But when we do, it's wonderful. And even if we don't, we can feel a shift, a change. That separate "I" may still be there, but some development has occurred. We're walking toward the ocean. We have dropped some things off because we realize we don't need the extra baggage.

When we traveled with Baba on his Third World Tour, each of us was allowed two suitcases. But we stayed in some places for six months. Staying in a place for that long, you accumulate things. So at the end of six months, you have to decide: "Okay, what can I let go of? Of all the things that don't fit inside my two suitcases, what don't I need?"

It is a process of elimination. You think, "Oh, that person really wanted me to have this thing..."

"Yes, but it doesn't fit in the suitcase."

So you say *svāhā*, you have to let it go.

As you do sādhanā, you go through a process that at first is filled with "I," "I," "I." Eventually you reach a place of greater understanding, and you ask yourself, "Who is this I?"

If you are asking from an expanded state, then even the question "Who am I?" disappears. Because there is no "I" to ask the question.

Question: Quite often in meditation, a lot of fear comes up and I don't know how to manage it. I was wondering if you could please talk a little bit about fear.

Gurudev: We had this question come up at the retreat just now. Again, we could say, that I, the cup, meets the ocean. And the cup doesn't yet want to become one with the ocean. Because the cup likes itself. So our fear is simply fear of the dissolution of the cup into the ocean.

If you allow yourself to merge drop by drop into the ocean, you realize there is no need to fear. Yet the fear is there. You experience, "If I dissolve, then who am I?"

Therefore, you engage in the process of understanding "Who am I?"

As you become established in that experience, the fear goes away. The cup is gone. You are part of the one.

So you have to talk to yourself when fear arises. Be able to laugh also, and say, "What is there actually to be afraid of?" There's nothing to be afraid of other than the fact that your limitations will be gone.

The people in your family or people with whom you work may be afraid when they think, "I might become somebody better. I might become somebody other." Because they like the identity they have created. The same thing happens with a seeker. Although mentally he understands everything is Consciousness, and he knows it's okay to be Consciousness, still he's not so sure the wave wants to give up its identity.

HOLD YOUR BLISS

Question: I can be in a state of bliss, but because the body is a transmitter and receiver of energy, if I pick up someone else's negative energy, I lose that bliss. What can I do?

Gurudev: In the state of bliss, you are wide open. The scriptures explain that when we are wide open, when we have not closed the gates, it is easy for other energies to penetrate our aura—if that is what you want to call it.

You have to learn that when someone else or something else comes along, you may need to reduce your energy field. You may need to contain your aura within certain limits so the other's energy does not penetrate you.

Hold the awareness of bliss within yourself, without making actual contact with that person. You are looking but not looking. By staying in that state of bliss, and not going out of it, you don't pick up the other influences.

Question: How can one find peace? How can the mind become immersed in divinity? Is there a technique?

Gurudev: All the things we did yesterday and today, and will do tomorrow and over the weekend, are techniques. We chant. We meditate. We keep good company. We read good things. We discard that which is useless.

As a seeker, the first thing to clarify within yourself is what is real and useful, and worth keeping. And tell adiós to whatever is not worth keeping.

Often people say, "I am letting go." But they haven't actually let go. One hand has let go, but the other hand is still holding it. They think, "I'm not so sure if I'm ready to be free of it." In true letting go, it's done. So be it.

There are many techniques for finding peace. But the point is not to get caught in the techniques. They must bear fruit. They must lead to an outcome.

Sometimes you meet somebody who is proud he has been on the path for X amount of years. But then you ask, "How far

have you gone on your journey?"
Just like our friend Mullah Nasruddin.
Nasruddin and his four friends took a row boat to an island. After they finished their party on the island, they got back in their boat and start rowing for home. By now it's the middle of the night. They are drunk, and they are rowing. The sun rises. Nasruddin and his friends find that they're still on the island. They forgot one thing: to untie the boat.
We do the same in life sometimes. We row and put forth great effort, but we go nowhere. Because of our ego, our attachment, and so many things, we are tied.
The very first thing is to free yourself. Then row. You will arrive at your destination.

Question: I am familiar with all the attachments I've got. It's not easy to pull away from some of them. I keep seeking new attachments in order to get to a new thrill.

Gurudev: I think we always look for a thrill. Especially in our society today, we look for the thrill outside ourselves.
What we want to do eventually is come to the realization that pleasure comes from the Self, not from the objects of enjoyment.
If all pleasure comes from the Self, we can ask, "Why does the Self become engaged in external objects of enjoyment? What need is there to indulge in sense pleasures?"
The Shaivite scriptures tell us, "The Self is perfect and satisfied in itself and has no need to indulge in sense pleasures, yet out of its own free will, it does enjoy the senses." This indulgence does not diminish or defile the Self. On the contrary, it enriches its experience all the more.
An example that is used in Shaivism is of a beautiful woman putting on ornaments. The woman is already beautiful, so the ornaments reflect her beauty. And in turn, they beautify her even more.
Of course, in this example, the ornaments are separate from

the woman. So her enjoyment is dependent on the external ornaments. In the case of the Self, however, the ornaments—the enjoyable objects—are manifestations of the Self. The Self is perfectly independent in its enjoyment of them.

This is the sport of the Self. The enjoyment of the world is seen as the free activity of the Self.

This is expressed in one of the *Śiva Sūtras* that Baba often quoted: *Lokānandah samādhi sukham*. "The bliss of the world is the bliss of samādhi."

I'm sure when you first hear this, you ask yourself, "How can external enjoyment be the same as samādhi, or immersion within?"

It can be the same because that joy—or thrill, as you said—doesn't come from the external object. It comes from within you.

LIVE IN THE WORLD AND PRACTICE YOGA

Question: How can I experience the union of yoga in everyday life?

Gurudev: You have to make yoga a part of life.

I always tell people, "Don't make life into compartments." When you create compartments, you have problems trying to fit everything in.

Become clear about who you are. Once you've become clear about who you are, take that individual through the day.

Yoga teaches us "See God in each other."

Yoga teaches us to be in touch with the divine within.

Yoga teaches us to be content at all times.

We can carry so many of the things yoga teaches with us into life. You may do your practices at one time, in one place. Yet you can carry the teachings with you everywhere, always.

I think to always be open and welcoming is wonderful.

Question: Is it enough for us, as householders, just to work on our own state, when we're surrounded by people who have made it clear they're not interested in meditation or yoga?

Gurudev: I think such people are great tools to help you to stay calm, centered, loving, kind, focused, compassionate. When you're with them, you have to do all the things you do in yoga, you just don't use yogic terms.

I often share that when you are with family and friends who are not interested in the path of yoga, all you have to do is love them more.

At some point, they ask you, "Why are you so nice to me?"

You simply tell them, "Because I love you."

Then one day, something in them wants to know, "Why is it that even when I don't want to talk to you or listen to you, you are still so nice to me?"

It is a great gift for us to be able to live in the world and practice yoga.

One of Baba's main messages, especially on his third world

tour, was to take the teachings and the practices into daily life. Don't just say, "I'm a great yogi" or "I'm at peace in the ashram." Rather, while living in the world, be peaceful. If you can still meditate, still do your practices, he would say, then you have really imbibed something.

Often people who follow the path become excited and want to share with their family or friends: "I have something that you should also do!"

But the family is not so sure. They say, "You're crazy!"

Of course, when we look at people who don't do what we are doing, we think they are crazy.

Imagine some people are in a room. They are starting to chant. Someone is playing the harmonium. Somebody else is playing the drum. When the chant gets going, people start to sway. Maybe some are dancing.

Now, a deaf person looks in through the window. He can't hear the music; he just sees the people moving. So he thinks, "Crazy people!"

The sages say that a person who doesn't practice yoga and hasn't heard the inner music doesn't understand what that is. To such a person, the idea of an inner experience seems crazy. But once they have experienced it, they think, "Wow."

So each of us has to find different ways to entice such people—not so much to come to an ashram or to satsaṅg, but to open up to themselves. They are closed to themselves in one way or another, so we have to find ways they can feel their own love, feel their own divinity, feel their own joy.

Question: How do you not fall into the trap of wanting to rescue them? How do you offer without attachment to this path?

Gurudev: Baba used to tell a story about a sage who had the mantra "That's why you are what you are."

The sage arrives at the palace of the king. He's stopped at the gate by the guard, and he tells the guard, "I want to meet the king."

The guard says, "Well, I can only take you to my supervisor."

The guard brings the sage to the supervisor. But the supervisor can only bring him to a low-level minister.

In each case, the sage says, "That's why you are what you are"—meaning that the limitation of the guard is that he can only take him to the supervisor, and the limitation of the supervisor is that he can only take him to a low-level minister, and the minister can only take him to the prime minister. The prime minister is the one who finally takes him to the king.

In Baba's story, each person's capacity is determined by the job he does. Of course, the lowest guard wants to be the prime minister. He thinks, "Then I could be with the king. I could advise the king. I could see who comes, and what each one says to the king." But he doesn't have the capacity within himself to be the prime minister, and therefore he's just the guard at the gate.

Similarly, as we go through life, we can't expect the same thing from each individual we meet. The capacity of each individual is only so much. We may want him to become a prime minister, but that's not in him. You have to realize that's the best that person can do. Therefore, there's no need to get upset or angry or attached.

When you serve people, you have to gauge the level of their understanding. Sometimes it just takes a little chat or even a simple question. The way they answer will tell you whether they are a guard or a supervisor or a low-level minister or the prime minister, or maybe even the king.

Another way to explain this is to say that we can't expect a little child to understand what a high school student would understand. We can't expect a high school student to understand what a university student would understand.

In life, one person is like a child, another is like a middle school student, another is like a high school student, and yet another is like a university student. Accordingly, although somebody's body may be fifty or sixty years old, his mentality may only be that of a child or a high school student.

Question: I work with people who are in a lot of pain, homeless, hungry, tired, and abused. Often I feel that nothing I might do is ultimately going to help them.

Gurudev: I think people who are homeless first need food and shelter. The second thing that helps is your love and your joy. Whenever I meet homeless people, I try to make them laugh or have fun. Usually, they can relate to that. If you try to talk to them about God, their response is, "What God?" Because they see God as the one who put them where they are. So they say, "I don't want that God."

But if your joy and love shine through, they start to wonder, "Why is this person so happy? Why is he always smiling, always laughing?" Maybe it takes a few years, but somewhere down the road they at least begin to contemplate what you have shown them.

You know, Baba was very quiet about what he gave people. He didn't go around saying, "I'm a Guru. I'm going to give God to you." He was who he was, and he did what he had to do. And just because he was who he was, people got what they had to get.

We all have our own karma. And it isn't possible to change somebody else's karma. No matter how much I want to help somebody, if that person has a certain understanding, then that is what his or her understanding will be.

People doing volunteer work sometimes approach it as a mission: "I'm going to do this, and I'm going to bring about change." A few years later, they feel disappointed because they realize, "I can't bring about change. I can only give, and whatever can be received from my giving will be received."

The main thing we can give others is acceptance. I don't mean just "this is where you are, so accept it." But loving and kind acceptance, so they can slowly learn to love and accept themselves.

In Shaivism, there is a sūtra that says, "One is called a *saṁsārin*, person of this world, who has enveloped himself in *dāridrya*."

No good English translation exists for dāridrya. You can think of it as poverty of śakti, of energy. Being poor in śakti binds one to this world. The purpose of yoga is to make one rich again—not in material wealth but in spiritual grace. Until one has spiritual wealth, one will not feel uplifted.

Recently, when we were in Houston, someone shared a story about one of his partners, who wanted to do something for people living on the street. When he saw a homeless person, he would hand out his card and say, "Come to my office, I'll give you a job."

Nobody ever showed up.

I think that whenever we do something for others with love, we should admit we do it because it gives us joy. We can say we do it because it will make the other person feel happy. But ultimately we are selfish; we do it because it gives us joy. We want to see them happy because that makes us happy.

A few years ago, in Haridwar, a bunch of us were coming back from the Ganges. We saw some people begging outside a restaurant, and decided to feed them. Everyone was in line, but a few got out of the line, saying things such as "Buy me flour, I don't eat at this restaurant" and "Give me a cup of tea, I don't want food."

So I said, "Wait, this is what we're giving. If you want the food, take it. If not, find somebody else."

One man in tattered orange robes said, "It's cold. I need a blanket!"

It was January, so I sent one of the boys who was with me to buy the man a blanket.

He told the boy, "Follow me."

The boy said, "No, I'm not going where you want to take me. We are going to a shop."

So the boy took him there and bought him a blanket. Later, he saw the same man following somebody else, again begging, "Give me a blanket, give me a blanket."

When we finished that day, as we were on our way back to the ashram, a man came running. He said, "Wait, I'm still here.

I need to be fed too!"

I said, "We've finished for today. I don't have any more money with me."

"Unless you feed me," he said, "whatever you have given today will be zero."

I said, "Well, too bad, I don't buy that." And I walked away. The man said a few choice words, and then went off and found somebody else.

So I think, in this kind of situation, you do the best you can. You can't feel pity. You can't feel sad. You simply give from your heart. You make sure your intentions are clear. And that's all you can do.

For example, if somebody is sick and keeps dwelling on "Oh, I'm so sick, I'm so sick," what can you do? You can't remove the person's mind, convince it "You're not sick," and put it back into the person. In a sense, you have to learn to become indifferent.

This is a predicament I find in the work I do.

People say, "I can't meditate."

I say, "Try this…"

Then I see them a few months later: "I still can't meditate."

"Well, I told you to do this..."

"Well, that doesn't work."

I remember somebody who came to me with the same problem every time. I always told her the same thing because I knew that would work. If only she had tried it! The last time she came, she posed a problem and said, "And don't tell me to do this…"

I said, "You know what you need to do."

I never saw her again.

People get into a groove, and they get stuck in it. Therefore, to me, even in the work I do, I've had to learn to be indifferent. One cannot be satisfied because somebody practices and lives what one teaches. Nor can one be disappointed because somebody else doesn't.

Everybody comes for different reasons. I noticed this around

Baba. Some people came because they loved to chant and meditate and do the practices. Some came and talked to him about politics or business. I would think, "You are with a great saint. Why do you want to waste your time?"

But as years went by, I realized that was all they knew, all they wanted. That was the extent of their capacity. If that was the only way they could receive grace—and if Baba was willing to listen to them—then that was fine.

Baba had great compassion. At the same time, he recognized that what he could give was limited by people's capacity.

The best example I can think of is that if you go to the ocean with a little cup, you will receive a cupful of water. If you go to the ocean with a bucket, you will receive a bucketful. Or you can throw yourself into the ocean and become part of it.

GLOSSARY

ābhāsavāda: seeing everything as a reflection
ācārya: revered teacher
Ādi Śaṅkarācārya: [788-820 CE] sage, originator of Advaita Vedānta
adhyāya: study
ahaṁkāra: ego
ājñā: the chakra of the third eye; literally, command
ānanda: bliss
aṅga-nyāsa: ritual for purification of parts of the body
āratī: waving of lights to worship a deity
Āratī Karūṅ: chant; literally, "Let us wave the lights"
Arjuna: a warrior, hero of the *Bhagavad Gītā*
āsana: yogic posture
āśrama: stage of life
Ātman: the soul, Self
avadhūta: ascetic
Āyurveda: the ancient Indian science of health
Bhagavad Gītā: Hindu scripture
bhakti: devotion
Bhakti Sūtras: scripture on divine love
bhasma: sacred ash
bhastrikā: type of prāṇāyāma; bellows breath
bhāva: feeling
bindu: dot
buddhi: intellect
chakra: energy center in the subtle body
Caṇḍī: one of the many forms of the Goddess
Chaitanya Mahāprabhu: [1486-1534] Bengali saint
Chinmāyānanda, Swami: [1916–1993], wrote commentary on the *Bhagavad Gītā*
cit: Consciousness
citta: the mind; subconscious mind
dāridrya: poverty consciousness
darśan: vision of the divine, experienced in the presence of a holy being
Daśanāmi: order of monks founded by Ādi Śaṅkarācārya;

literally, ten names
Devī: the Goddess
dharma: right action, righteous law
Gaṇeśa: elephant-headed god, son of Śiva, remover of obstacles
gopī: devotee of Kṛṣṇa
guṇa: one of the three qualities in nature
Guru Gītā: commentary on the Guru
Hare Rāma Hare Kṛṣṇa: chant to Rāma and Kṛṣṇa, incarnations of the God Viṣṇu
Haṁsa: mantra; literally, "I am That"
hṛdaya: heart
jaḍ: inert
japa: repetition of a mantra
jayanti: birthday
Jñāneśvar Mahārāj: [13th c.] poet-saint of Maharashtra
Jyota se Jyota: chant invoking the Guru's grace
Kabīr: [1440-1518] poet-saint and weaver
Kali Yuga: the dark age, the last of four ages
Kankhal: village near Haridwar, India, where a Shanti Mandir ashram is located
kara-nyāsa: ritual for purification of the hands
Kashmir Shaivism: philosophy based on the idea that all is Consciousness
Kaṭha Upaniṣad: a Hindu scripture
Krishnamurti, Jiddu: [1895-1986] philosopher
kriyā: mental or physical purification, generated by the awakened kuṇḍalinī
kriyamana: karma done in this life
Kṛṣṇa: Hindu deity, Guru of Arjuna in the *Bhagavad Gītā*
Kulārṇava Tantra: tantric scripture
kumbhaka: retention of breath
Kumbh Melā: vast gathering of sādhus and pilgrims
kuṇḍala: coil
kuṇḍalinī: spiritual energy dormant within all humans, can be awakened by the Guru

laddu: ball-shaped Indian sweet
Lalitā Sahasranāma: thousand names of the Goddess
loka: place, world
Magod: village in Gujarat, India, where a Shanti Mandir ashram is located
Mahābhārata: Hindu scripture, contains the *Bhagavad Gītā*
Mahāmandaleshwar: a distinguished teacher in the Śaṅkarācārya order of monks
mahāsamādhi: final merging with the Absolute
manana: contemplation
manas: mind
manasa pūjā: mental worship
mantra: sacred words or syllables, literally "that which protects the mind"
mala: impurity
mālā: a string of beads used like a rosary
mātṛkā: power behind the letters of a word or mantra
māyā: illusion
māyīya: limited
Nāciketa: boy hero of *Kaṭha Upaniṣad*
Nasruddin, Mullah: Sufi folk character
Navrātra: nine-night celebration of the Goddess
nididhyāsana: absorption
nirvikalpa: beyond attribute, thought, or image
Oṁ Namaḥ Śivāya: mantra; literally, "I bow to the divine"
Pādukā Pañcakam: five stanzas on the Guru's sandals
Pārvatī: Hindu goddess, wife of Śiva
Patañjali: [2nd c BCE] author of the Yoga Sūtras
prāṇa: the life breath
prāṇāyāma: regulation of the breath
prārabdha: karma from a former life that manifests in this lifetime
Pratyabhijñāhṛdayam: 11th c. text on Kashmir Shaivism
pratyāhāra: withdrawal of the senses
pūjā: worship
rajas: the quality of passion

Rāma: incarnation of Lord Viṣṇu
Rām Tīrth, Swami: [1873-1906] Indian saint
Rudram: chant praising Rudra
sādhanā: spiritual practices
sādhu: a mendicant
sahasrāra: the crown chakra (energy center)
śakti: the creative energy of the universe; the awakened spiritual energy
śaktipat: transmission of śakti by the Guru
samādhi: union with the Absolute
sampradāya: tradition
saṁsārin: a person subject to the cycle of death and rebirth
saṁskāra: latent impression
sanātan: universal, eternal
sañcita: karma collected over lifetimes
sandhyā: transitions, dawn and dusk
Śaṅkara: name for Śiva
sannyāsa: renunciation
satsaṅg: in the company of the Truth
sattva: the quality of purity
savikalpa: with thoughts remaining
sevā: selfless service to the Guru
siddha: perfected master
Śiva: Hindu deity, the primordial Guru
Śiva Mahimnaḥ Stotram: hymn in praise of Śiva
Śivarātri: the night of Śiva
Śiva Sūtras: 9th c. text of Kashmir Shaivism
smṛti: that which is remembered
śraddhā: faith
śravaṇa: listening
Śrī Chakra: symbolic representation of the Goddess
Śrī Rām: chant to Lord Rāma, incarnation of Lord Viṣṇu
śruti: that which is heard
sūrya namaskār: salutations to the sun, hatha yoga posture
suṣumnā: major channel in the subtle body
sūtra: aphorism, verse

sva: self
svādhyāya: self-study
svāhā: so be it, literally, "I surrender it to the Self"
tamas: the quality of darkness and inertia
tāmasika: having a dark quality
tattva: principle
Tukārām Mahārāj: [1608-1650] poet-saint
turīya: fourth state of consciousness, state of oneness
Uddhava: friend of Kṛṣṇa in the *Bhāgavata Purāṇa*
ujjāyī: type of prāṇāyāma with forced out-breath
Upaniṣads: ancient Hindu scriptures
Vasiṣṭha: Vedic sage
Vedānta: philosophy based on the *Vedas*
Vedas: ancient Hindu scriptures
viśala: magnanimous
viveka: discrimination between the real and the unreal
vṛtti: modification of the mind
yajña: fire ritual
Yama: god of death
Yoga Sūtras: scripture compiled by Patañjali
Yudhiṣṭhira: eldest Pāṇḍava brother in the *Mahābhārata*

MAHĀMANDALESHWAR SWAMI NITYĀNANDA

Mahāmandaleshwar Swami Nityānanda is from a lineage of traditional spiritual teachers in India. While carrying the traditional teachings, he makes spirituality a practical part of modern daily reality, guided by the prayer "May all beings live in peace and contentment."

Born in 1962, Swami Nityānanda was raised from birth in an environment of yoga and meditation. His parents were devotees of the famous ascetic *avadhūta* Bhagavān Nityānanda, and then became disciples of his successor, the renowned Guru Baba Muktānanda.

Swami Nityānanda was trained from childhood by Baba Muktānanda and initiated into the mysterious path of the Siddha Gurus. He learned the various yogic practices, including meditation and Sanskrit chanting, and studied the philosophies of Vedānta and Kashmir Shaivism.

He was initiated into the Sarasvatī order of monks in 1980 at eighteen years of age and was given the name Swami Nityānanda by Baba Muktānanda. In 1981, Baba Muktānanda declared Swami Nityānanda would succeed him to carry on the lineage.

In 1987, Swami Nityānanda founded Shanti Mandir as a vehicle for continuing his Guru's work and subsequently established four ashrams.

In 1995, at the age of thirty-two, at a traditional ceremony in Haridwar, India, the ācāryas and saints of the Daśnām tradition installed him as a Mahāmandaleshwar of the Mahānirvani Akhara. He is the youngest recipient since the inception of this order.

Currently Swami Nityānanda, also known as Gurudev, travels around the world, sharing the spiritual practices in which he has been trained.

Mahāmandaleshwar Swami Nityānanda

SHANTI MANDIR

Shanti Mandir, a spiritual nonprofit organization, is dedicated to the propagation of Baba Muktānanda's teachings.

One of the ashrams of Shanti Mandir is near the banks of the River Ganges, at Kankhal, near Haridwar. The ashram at Magod is in rural surroundings, amidst a twenty-acre mango orchard, in the state of Gujarat. The third ashram in India is adjacent to the samādhi shrine of Bhagavān Nityānanda, in the village of Ganeshpuri, in Maharashtra state. Shanti Mandir's ashram in the United States is on 294 wooded acres outside the town of Walden, New York.

Under the guidance of Swami Nityānanda, Shanti Mandir symbolizes peace, progress, and love. In addition to the spiritual practices carried on daily, these ashrams contribute their resources toward the following charitable activities: Śrī Muktānanda Sanskrit Mahāvidyālaya (education), Shanti Arogya Mandir (health), and Shanti Hastkala (economic upliftment through handicrafts).

Baba Muktānanda

Bhagavān Nityānanda

LOKĀḤ SAMASTĀḤ SUKHINO BHAVANTU

MAY ALL BEINGS BE CONTENT

www.ingramcontent.com/pod-product-compliance
Lightning Source LLC
Chambersburg PA
CBHW052011290426
44112CB00014B/2202